THE EUROPEAN REPUBLIC

Centre de Sciences Humaines (Centre for Social Sciences and Humanities): Created in New Delhi in 1989 the CSH, is part of network of research centres of the French Ministry of Foreign Affairs. The Centre's research work is primarily oriented towards the study of issues concerning the contemporary dynamics of development in India and South Asia. The activities of the Centre are focused on four main themes, namely: Economic growth and sustainable development, International and regional relations, Institutional structures and political constructions of identity and Urban dynamics.

(Centre de Sciences Humaines, 2 Aurangzeb Road, New Delhi 110011, India - Tel: (91 11) 301 62 59/ 301 41 73 - Fax: (91 11) 301 84 80 - E-mail: public@csh-delhi.com - Website: http://www.csh-delhi.com)

Institute Français de Pondichéry (French Institute of Pondicherry): Created in 1955, the IFP is a multidisciplinary research and advanced educational institute. Major research works are focusing on Sanskrit and Tamil languages and literatures—in close collaboration with the *Ecole Française d'Extrême- Orient*—ecosystems, biodiversity and sustainability, dynamics of population and socio-economic development.

(Institute Français de Pondichéry, 11, Saint Louis Street, P.B. 33 Pondicherry 605 001 - Tel.: (91 413) 334 170/334 168 - Telex: 469224 FRAN-In, Fax: (91 413) 339 534 - E-mail: instfran@giasmd01.vsnl.net.in - Website: http: www.ifpindia. org)

The European Republic

MICHEL FOUCHER

MANOHAR

CENTRE DE SCIENCES HUMAINES
2002

French edition published by
Belin, Paris, 1998
2nd edition 2000

First published in English in 2002
Translated from French by Saroj Butani

ISBN 81-7304-430-9

Published by
Ajay Kumar Jain for
Manohar Publishers & Distributors
4753/23 Ansari Road, Daryaganj
New Delhi 110 002

Typeset by
Kohli Print
Delhi 110 051

Printed at
Lordson Publishers Pvt. Ltd.
Delhi 110 007

Contents

Preface

THIS is the English version of the work which under the original French title, *La République européenne*, was published in November 2000. It has already been translated into several languages, these being Hungarian, Estonian, Serbian and Russian and is currently being translated into German, Polish, Rumanian and Mandarin Chinese, among others.

The present work is meant for the English-speaking readers of the Indian Union in particular, and those of South Asian countries in general, which is a regional group in the process of formation, full of promise once the contentious issues of the recent past have been overcome to give place to a common innovative project. The book aims at bringing an awareness about the bases of the European project which I have positioned within the category of a 'republic', a word that has come from the Latin '*respublica*', not in order to indicate an institutional configuration, a sort of complete federation into which nations would enter in reduced strength, but to mark out the geopolitical originality of the European Union in the process of its construction. To refresh the memory, to reconstruct a heritage, to revive History. In so doing I draw my inspiration from the thought processes of my friend Shashi Tharoor, who holds a high position in the office of the Secretary General of the United Nations. He is the author of the remarkable *The Great*

Indian Novel. To write for those who are not able to distinguish their *kundalini* (vital force of cosmic energy embodied within each of us and portrayed as a coiled serpent at the base of the spinal column) from a decaying earthworm. This then is what this personal essay strives to convey.

Europeans are eager for unity in order to overcome the risks arising out of their diversity. Earlier centuries have shown the magnitude of the nationalist, ideological and imperialist tragedies that Europeans were capable of enacting. It is this admission which has constituted its starting point.

Respublica, therefore, is in response to the Republic of Letters in the Europe of the Age of Enlightenment, the one which the eighteenth century witnessed, when no cultural police drew border lines shutting out the free circulation of the ideas and values of progress. *Respublica* is viewed as an affirmation of citizenship, since religious, ethnic and philosophic affiliations were treated, in France and elsewhere, as personal matters, the State guaranteeing the equality, the fraternity—the solidarity, in contemporary language—and the freedom, of citizens. *Respublica* once again can be discerned in the essence of 'public thing', which I translate as 'public good', that which our forefathers were able to build, in the wake of the long European civil war which lasted in fact from 1933 to 1945, and of which we are, in the year 2001, both the heirs and the accountants.

In this aspect, the political face of the Republic contrasts, in European history, with that of the Empire. Indeed, a large part of the history of European States can be summarized as being a struggle between some States which, at a given moment, have attempted to impose their hegemony on other European States, and the reaction of the latter, forced to forge coalitions in order to put hurdles in the way of the former. The project of the European Community was born out of the awareness of the tragic deadlock resulting from these struggles for hegemony on European soil. Most of the States involved in the common adventure have been able to confirm this only by giving up their empires. The European construction is contemporaneous to the failure of the European projects for empires, as well as to decolonization.

The European Union according to its founding fathers, Jean Monnet and Robert Schuman, is a novel and step by step attempt at overstepping the contradictions inherent in the free interplay of national interests through the establishment of 'real solidarities' between old Nation States, proud of being such. This adventure has been continuing for more than half a century and, contrary to forebodings of mischance, it has not only survived the generally peaceful end to a contained and bipolar disorder, but it has made a peaceful transition possible on the European continent, with the cruel exception of the western Balkans. The European Union is a 'success story' and it is from this that its present difficulties arise, as it has now to initiate a new phase of integration of institutions, a redefinition of the modalities of collective decision, an extension towards Central and Eastern Europe of the gains of the European Community. All this has not been easy but as will be seen very shortly in the coming years, we are capable of meeting the challenges. Teething troubles there may have been, but in no event has there been an undermining of a model which has proved its worth by conciliating the exercise of the sovereignty of nations together with respect for solidarities between States whose national interests have coalesced.

Surmounting national antagonisms and laying the bases for a realistic cooperation is time consuming. Europe has no lesson to teach the world but its specific experience is deserving of attention. Proof is now available that it is possible to combine the pursuit of legitimate national interests and also take into account those of the neighbours, in a match which no longer ends in a draw. Hence the progress in the fields of the single market, the single currency from 1 January 2002 and, beyond that, of joint defence, capable of managing national crises in the near neighbourhood, and even a foreign policy—not single like the currency, but at least joint—based on shared analyses, exchanged perceptions, convergent approaches.

Europe today is not synonymous with uniformity. Its wealth is based on pluralism, on the diversity of its people and its cultures, as the French Prime Minister, Lionel Jospin, recalled with strength of conviction, in his speech on 28 May 2001, in Paris, on the future of an enlarged Europe. Conciliating the unity of political action with the diversity of the nations that this community is composed of, this is its constant wager. This is also the response that organized Europe can make to the growing challenges, to the uniformization of the world, to the age of globalization, which some look upon as being inevitable.

Democracy is neither agreement nor consensus but the art of

managing disagreements in a civilized manner, which implies respecting the otherness inherent in all collective geopolitical construction. It does not behove me to point out here what the European Union can draw out of the experiences of the Indian Union and reciprocally, nor what the European Union, in the process of enlargement, extending its hands towards other nations finally freed from the Soviet domination, can mean for the future of South Asia.

I remain however convinced that we can go beyond the age of power equations alone and of the refusal to settle quarrels between neighbours, by setting in place bold projects of cooperation. When the French Minister for Foreign Affairs, Mr Hubert Védrine, gave a speech at the India International Centre in New Delhi in March 1999, in the company of his colleague Mr Jaswant Singh, at the closing session of an Indo-French seminar on the theme of multipolarity, he gave the call for the formation of a 'cooperative multipolarity', of which Europe and India, among others, could become the promoters. May this work inspire reflection on this joint task, for the European Union and South Asia.

Paris/Lyon
June 2001

MICHEL FOUCHER

INTRODUCTION

Europe, a New World?

The constructs of futurologists can only be verified in a world in which no happening of importance occurs.

HANNAH ARENDT (*Du mensonge à la violence*, 1972)

EUROPE, a province of the relational world, is a continent par excellence in which doubt and self-criticism form the edifice of the discourse of Europeans on themselves. This philosophic bent of mind delineates an original trait of their personality, attaching as it does, great value to the primacy of an individual and the freedom to act, to believe and to judge.

If one were to be satisfied with the way things were going, if everything was stable all around, if the structure was complete, the objective achieved, autonomous power finally acquired and brought under control, in short, if one were to cease to doubt and to give free rein to paradoxical propositions, would one still be 'European'? The completed state of affairs would be fatal to Europe for it is precisely this state of tension, this endeavour constantly being refashioned, this desire for Europe, this construction whose final pattern remains unknown, that appears to be the only worthwhile cause.

It has always seemed to me that among thinkers, it is philosophers who are the most competent to write on the subject of Europe. Accustomed as they are to the vast categories of reason, endowed with a broad vision extending over twenty-five centuries at least, spanning the course followed by Europeanity from the time of Aristotle to, let us say, Vladimir Jankélévitch and Jürgen Habermas, they have been undoubtedly the first to ponder over this matter.

After them, in the order of precedence of the *académie*, would come historians who, bringing the past into the present, impose upon themselves the wisdom to distance themselves from the moment in time which assails us, to place it in the long term perspective. Indeed Europe, as the eminent historian Jacques Le Goff has said, is not old but 'ancient', like a substructure. I hence deduce from this, by way of hypothesis, that Europe cannot profess to be an 'old continent'. If we are to believe this, how can we imagine the future if not in the form of a patrimonial or a nostalgic conservation? Is Europes a museum of endeavours in the face of America, which daily reiterates its status as a continent that is new, turned towards the future, while having also incessantly to contend with an introvert and regressive moralism?

In this scholarly areopagus, which also gathers within its fold painters, musicians and poets, geographers are the underlings who appear as intruders, or worse, who play supporting roles. Moreover, unlike history, represented by Clio, they have no muse assigned to them. Culture is not their primary domain, and with some rare exceptions, the long duration on which they base their work appears too extensive, too geological, to be human. They have to work, therefore, through borrowed learning, or else, like Atlas, advance relentlessly into unknown spheres, hoping to find a key which will open the door to concrete interpretations. They have at least the merit of not being carried away by nostalgia, being stimulated instead, as a result of the scientific side of their nature, by the meticulous observation of facts and by complex correlationships.

Does the geographer play a role in European scholarship? Scholars teach us to display the same concern for surveys which the administrators of ancient China showed. Land registers, hydraulic surveys, minute cartographies of provinces and cities were matters that preoccupied the minds of Chinese administrators far ahead of the inventories made by the Europeans of the Renaissance. Nevertheless, in the past, European geographers were able to conduct investigations—the original meaning of the Greek word 'history'—and to ponder over the vast divisions of the world in the form of climate, rivers, customs, continents and borders. Their action was already one of differentiation. After the Renaissance, in a period of objectivity emancipated from theology, they devised depictions which fed the imagination and sketched the icons of our identities. These can be admired in the powerful and intriguing painting of Vermeer de Delft *Le Géographe* (1669), forming a counterpart to *L'Astronome* (1668): with maps covering the walls, the scientist is seen glancing turned towards the horizon, circumscribed by the window frame, the source of light and enlightenment. In an earlier painting, which illustrates the cover of the work *L'art de la peinture* (1662–7), we observe an artist, his back towards us, in a workshop. He is painting History, portrayed by the muse Clio, against the background of Geography, represented here by a map of the Dutch United Provinces in which the North is to the right, and which bears the inscription '*nova descriptio*', a clear reference to Ptolemy. An admirable depiction of the hoary dialogue between time and space! Just as the Dutch painters of the Golden Age tried to capture a whole range of knowledge and information about the world on their canvas (*Vermeer, mystère du quotidien*, by Rémy Knafou, Herscher, 1994), geographers acquired, by means of the map, the right to approach the world in all its diversity and singularity. It was also through them that from the middle of the fifteenth century, the words 'Europe' and 'Europeans' were engraved on the first modern maps, enabling princes and humanists to view a remarkable portrayal of a continent. Following Gerardus Mercator and Jodocus Hondius, Europe was presented both as the smallest part of the world and as a nucleus, extending from Hispania to Moscovia, separated from Asia by Tartaria. Once it had acquired a tangible shape, this configuration was able to free itself from its origin in religion, which had been its characteristic on the '*Designatio orbis christiani*'.

Geographers have learnt, after philosophers, the role of perceptions and of portrayals, for bringing a corrective to the arrogance of objectivity. Along with historians, they were initiated into the dialectics of events and long durations, into the play of contingencies and permanencies: the only guarantee against determinism. Today they have to apply their minds to variations, to strata, to legacies, which are the intimations inscribing in space the effects of time in order, and by doing so, to discern the meaning they may embody. Johan Blaeu's introduction to his twelve-volume atlas of the world (*Le Grand Atlas*, Amsterdam, 1663, dedicated to the king

Louis XIV), confirms this link: '*Geography* [is] *the eye and the light of history*'.

I readily visualize European nations as the great figures of a classical painting in which each one stands out clearly against the background, but in which the totality derives its harmony from its structure, in accordance with a 'vanishing point', in the true meaning of the term, a 'perspective'. 'Europe' is the word which denotes this perspective, giving a significance to the whole, if indeed the exploit does withstand the ravages of time.

A GEOGRAPHER'S JOURNEY

Europe occupied but a tiny place in the mind of a geographer whose theoretical learning was acquired on the benches of the Sorbonne at the end of the sixties and whose practical work was conducted on the research sites in what has been magnified under the term 'Third World'. This phrase was an abstract but eloquent concept for an inhabitant of a 'First World', both certain of his prosperity and sometimes overcome by doubt, over the origin of this economic and moral comfort.

During this period, the France of de Gaulle had been able to secure for itself, within the strategic comfort of the cold war, a space of independent expression in which it was thought that even a simple posture and the obvious potency of the spoken word would suffice to change the face of the world. France, to exist, it was then vaunted, needed the presence of no European detour. This was the time when Franco-German reconciliation was being endorsed—de Gaulle delivered memorable speeches in German which he had learnt by heart—Adenauer paid a visit to Reims. The famous General had naturally been able, once again, to forestall others by formulating a durable concept, but which was interpreted out of context for too long. Breaking away from the political geography dictated by the cold war, he proposed that 'a European solidarity be created extending from the Atlantic to the Urals'. His objective was to point out to the leaders of the Soviet Union that the European Community decided upon in 1957 was not aimed at heightening the spirit of confrontation—the Cuban crisis was still fresh in people's minds—but that it remained an open historical process. This historical foresight concealed another one which, for its part, has come into being and comprises the veritable premonition of the French leader. 'For this Europe to become possible, great changes are required. First of all, that the Soviet Union should no longer be what it is, but be Russia', he had said. This was a twice classical remark coming from this practitioner of history for whom it was not the Soviet Union, a transitory form of Russia, but indeed the Russian nation, which constituted a permanent reality. What was also classical was this image of the European continent which, since Vidal de la Blache at least and the series of maps which have adorned the walls of classrooms, found its 'natural', orographical border in the Ural mountains.

This new projection was the counterpart of another spatial metaphor, this one established in keeping with a meridian axis. We barely recall this image of France, extending from Dunkirk to Tamanrasset, which was the first and briefly conceived geopolitical project proposed to the French. The geographic symmetry of these two concepts indicates fairly well that it was the function of one to succeed the other, which had become obsolete due to the realities of the emancipation of the Algerian nation. It was, moreover by giving up Algeria—that is to say imperialism—that France made its choice in favour of Europe, a happy substitute. Churchill had understood this already in 1944, when he asserted that 'colonies are no longer today a sign of good fortune nor a token of power'.

At this period, therefore, the other Europe was hardly of interest to anyone but geographers close to the communist left. This militant support served as a kind of sanction for conducting research in places as exotic as the Soviet Union, East Germany or Rumania, considered as the laboratories of true socialism, those in which the man-nature dialectics seemed to find its solution in favour of the first, to the greater satisfaction of former students of geomorphology courses. To those who entertained some reservations over these achievements of demiurges with iron fists while still harbouring a sense of solidarity towards them, the Third World offered a field of choice. One could study there the symptoms of underdevelopment and its effects in space; track down the scars of dependency; and analyze the strategies adopted by centres of insurrection. In short, in this setting, Europe was absent since a competition was taking place on a planetary scale between Moscow and Washington and the most lucid among researchers were hoping for a third path: hence the immense impact of the experience of the Popular Unity Government in Chile, the distant intimation of an alternative political scenario awaited by some for one or another State of Southern Europe.

THINKING OUT THE EVENT

It was only with the violent intrusion of the real in the form of 'the event', defined by Hannah Arendt as 'an unprecedented form that history gives rise to' and 'a place where new political issues emerge'—in this case the bifurcations of 1989–92—that Europe became once again a matter of scientific and educational interest for some geographers: a new world to be rediscovered had come into being.

Strangely enough, it was more this other Europe (labelled Eastern Europe), requiring to be rediscovered, which called into question the simplistic usage of the toponym Europe, and awakened interest, rather than the six-nation, the nine-nation or the twelve-nation Europe. Some works mark the dates of this renewed interest which was also an intellectual necessity: *Fragments d'Europe* (Michel Foucher), in 1993, as also the last volume of the *Géographie universelle*, '*Asie du Nord, Europe de l'Est*' (Roger Brunet and Violette Rey), in 1996, *L'Europe entre Maastricht et Sarajevo* (Armand Frémont, 1996), and DATAR, the Delegation's ambitious prospective programme for town and country planning and regional action. At the start of the decade, we knew in fact, more about the Chinese path of development, the affinity of Japan with the sea or the agricultural belts of the American plains than about the urban dynamics of Eastern Europe, the regional geography of the Ukraine or the interplay of minorities and borders in the Eastern bloc, a subject that was then a taboo. It was a welcome move that had come none too soon.

Nevertheless, this rediscovery did not suffice to make the changing face of Europe a subject for study. The attempts made to present the actual geography of Europe, that of the entire sum of the States of the European Union, as also that of the continent in the process of reconstitution, are still rare. The geographer, Jean-François Drevet, was able to tackle the issue, by dismantling the system of the strata which make of the greater Europe an accumulation of 'areas'—economy, institutions, crises, security, market (*L'identité européenne*, 1997). Michael Emerson sketched a problematic of Europe (*Redrawing the Map of Europe*, 1996). DATAR instituted a reflection on the new geoeconomy of the Union, encountering many difficulties as regards method and sources, and analysed the mutations on the scale of the continent (Michel Foucher and Jean-Yves Potel, *Le continent retrouvé*, 1993). The imperative of widening the Union from the point of view of the future extension of its structural foundations, led the European Commission (DG XVI) to undertake a study of strengths and weaknesses of the lands of the candidate countries. The multiplication of the steps for regional cross-border cooperation finally focused sharply on the dead angles of the cold war, from the Barents Sea to the Black Sea, and thereafter for other reasons, to the vicinity of the Caspian Sea.

The geographical approach was also sought by the French regalian ministries in an attempt to throw light on the conflicts motivated by some among the leading groups which had chosen to turn away from the struggle between classes to the struggle between peoples. Never before had so many maps been seen to explain conflicts and to suggest solutions than during the breaking out of the civil and national wars, pitting the Slavs of the south against each other.

Confining geographical analysis to the study of open or latent crises would amount to viewing it in a very simplistic and fairly grim manner. It is undoubtedly the easy way to consider geopolitics, the critical face of geography, as a science of territorial conflicts and contradictory portrayals. True, many crises remain unsolved as long as the territorial phantasms, in their archaism, are considered of prime importance, since they lock the players in a game always ending in a draw. Hence the disquieting but inevitable reappearance of the issue of borders. However there is a narrower but more promising way which consists in viewing applied geographical analysis from the perspective of an interaction between nations leading to a game with a positive outcome. What has admittedly been called 'European construction'—we will show further on the present limits of this metaphor—proceeds from a game having a positive outcome, like at the end of a negotiation concluding in a 'win win' situation with benefits accruing to all parties concerned.

Geographers are probably less at ease with this kind of process than economists, historians and, above all jurists. They attempt—and this is particularly true of the experts—to approach Europe, the object, in terms of competition between territories. In France, a case study widely perused since the time of German reunification, showed the consequences on French territory, of an inescapable 'displacement of Europe's centre of gravity towards the east' (*sic*)—France losing forever the centrality that it occupied in a twelve-nation Europe. The metaphor of the 'blue banana', removing the Ile-de-France, the North, the East and the Rhône-Alps, away from the backbone of a European nucleus in the form of an isthmus from London to Milan, led only towards strengthening this fear. This was further amplified by the elect of the riverside territories of the Atlantic or the Mediterranean, in search of financial compensations for purposes of achieving a balance. This imagery of French origin comprised, for a long time, the geographic view of the new Europe, even though the French territory is among the best endowed and the most productive in Europe and the Ile-de-France ranks foremost among the hundred and ninety-three regions of Europe in terms of production value.

This difficulty is again encountered when we ponder over the European geography being taught in the new French school courses (those at the start of the 1998 school year) revolving around the theme of power. While one of the public justifications for the making of Europe is precisely the need for constructing an autonomous pole of influence, by way of a single currency, which, as we all know, is currently being set up, in a world in a state of flux, presented as being multipolar, our school syllabi prefer to stick to the classic view of national domination. Hence the decision to teach about Germany in the geography class (general sections of Standard VI), while no specific chapter is devoted to the geography of European construction. When we consider the extent to which the images of the world get fixed in the mind during these formative years—note the craze for the 'Newly Industrialised Countries' (NIC) of Asia, which were a classic subject for the school leaving certificate, which later influenced the imagery of many decision makers among economists—one cannot but wonder at the discrepancies between the spatial changes that the history of the European nations is undergoing and the scanty mention these find in the syllabi.

It is of course difficult to freeze within texts meant for educational purposes, the description of a history in the making. One can also underline the pre-eminence of the historian's discourse, since in the case of France, almost 80 per cent of the history and geography teachers in schools and colleges are historians by training. It is at the same time a major intellectual asset for France to be able to harmoniously articulate these two approaches even if it signifies the 'depoliticisation' of geographers' knowledge. But that period is now in the past. One may also raise the objection that the works of reference relating to the new geography of Europe, notably those brought out by the Union, are still insufficient to constitute a basic corpus. The works already mentioned do, however, open up some fertile ground provided one takes the risk of disengaging oneself from strictly national frameworks.

GEOGRAPHY AND THE EUROPEAN REPUBLIC

From this assertion, it is evident that it is imperative for geographers to undertake a work of reappropriation or of reconstruction of Europe, the object. Historians took this task upon themselves during past periods, as is testified by the monumental work of Norman Davies (*Europe, A History*, 1996). The beginnings of European integration, during the 1950s, are now becoming a matter for historical analysis and, (a paradox that can be explained by a distanced scepticism in the face of the object) the most fertile are the British researchers (a good synthesis of this can be read in *The Question of Europe*, 1997, by Peter Gowan and Perry Anderson). The discretion of French historians on this same period is astonishing. It may be explained by a secret reticence of the guardians of national history faced with changed allegiances, while medievalists, on account of the object of their study, penetrate straight into a contemporary subject on which they can throw some helpful light (Jacques Le Goff, *La vieille Europe et la nôtre*, 1994).

For geographers, the wager is not simply one on the school or university level. It is already being contemplated that students be familiarized with the Euro while awaiting that they in turn initiate their more reticent parents, as they are already doing with home computers. But schools cannot be reduced to the level of technical learning. Another wager is the more directly civic one.

Geographers should be asked to break their silence to come out and participate in the inevitable debate on the making of Europe, particularly of the Union, which gives rise to very cautious and even conformist official views. Thus, can one remain satisfied with contemplating, without batting an eyelid, that the Union can shortly double its strength in members and continue to consider this as nothing but a change in numbers? Is it wise to consider that the introduction of the Euro would have no territorial consequences? Is it reasonable to put off *sine die* any public debate on the question of the final borders of Europe? Should we continue to justify European construction by the central but outdated arguments put forward by the founding fathers? Should we resolve to see in Europe nothing but a province on an implacable march towards 'globalisation'? Is there not a (social, geopolitical, environmental) European 'model' to be analysed and, if it exists, to be promoted, so that each one would convince himself that Europeans still have something to say?

This essay attempts to answer these queries. Its very title reveals its intention: to consider Europe as a '*respublica*', that is to say a 'shared property', a heritage, above all a place for invention of novel forms which could become more explicitly political. Its conception is, therefore, not patrimonial in the way that was meant by great authors who are glibly quoted.

The very word 'Europe' induces reflection since everyone uses it, in different places, to indicate different visions or projects. Its polysemia is akin to the political and national diversity of Europe. Its recurrence indicates sufficiently the 'power of a name', which needs to be pondered upon. This jointly owned property does not aim to replace the national republics that it wishes to encompass. The last decade has shown adequately enough the central role occupied by national affiliations and no one thinks today, even in those circles most attracted towards federalism, of 'constructing' a Europe opposed to nations. But a certain level of affiliation should be devised which is supra-national, functioning as a common reference, a little along the lines in which the philosophers of the Age of Enlightenment contemplated Europe as a 'respublica litterarum', a republic of letters, a space for the free circulation of new ideas, concept which faded away with nineteenth century nationalisms.

There are, nevertheless, some places where this spirit of '*Universitas*' does waft anew, a spirit that Michel Serres has described as being the earliest sign of a body being given to the idea of Europe. This was the experiment in the form of the College of Europe created in Bruges in 1950, in the wake of the Congress of Europe held in 1948, in the Hague, where almost 800 participants from around twenty countries met, just three years after the defeat of a pan-European project motivated by fascist and dictatorial trends.

Almost two thousand participants celebrated its fiftieth anniversary at the Hague in May 1998. However, no truly innovative message was voiced, except for the call for a 'European government and a constitutional pact' of a Union more clearly defined as being federal. But it constitutes an intermediary transit point for future generations.

Since 1994, there emerged a second campus of the College of Europe, situated at Natolin, a suburb of Warsaw. One hundred students from thirty European countries study here for a year in a series of buildings, some of which were earlier a part of the royal palace of Wilanow. While the working languages and medium of instruction are English and French, an average of almost half the students are proficient in four languages; the teaching is imparted in French, English and German. Norwegians and Portuguese rub shoulders with Moldavians and Estonians, while lectures are delivered by a horde of visiting professors coming from half a dozen countries. This college (where a fraction of hard-liners of the Polish Communist Party formerly plotted their intrigues) will gradually expand to admit two hundred and fifty students originating from the near totality of the member countries of the Union and from the majority of the candidate countries as well as from other States that are members of the Council of Europe. They will be trained to shoulder responsibilities in a new spirit, as has been done with the five thousand former students at Bruges. In the two campuses, the teachers are as nomadic as the humanists of the Renaissance and the scholars of the Middle Ages. English and French have replaced Latin and are opening up a border-free space for knowledge and communication.

By laying stress on approaches which promote the free movement of students and teachers in the spirit of the travels of scholars during the Middle Ages and the Renaissance—Erasmus, Socrates, etc.—the Commission knew that it would be contributing towards promoting the maintenance of a shared cultural wealth, through the intermixing of cultures and the meeting of individualities. A new '*Respublica*' of the arts, letters and sciences is coming into being before our very eyes.

Population of Europe and surrounding areas

Density of population

- 200
- 100
- 50

Urban areas

- more than 5 million inhabitants
- 1 to 5 million inhabitants

The new monetary nucleus

Euro 12 European Union

headquarters of the financial agencies linked to the EU

BERD
European Bank
for Reconstruction and Development

EIB
European Investment Bank

The Vatican is examing the adoption of the Euro

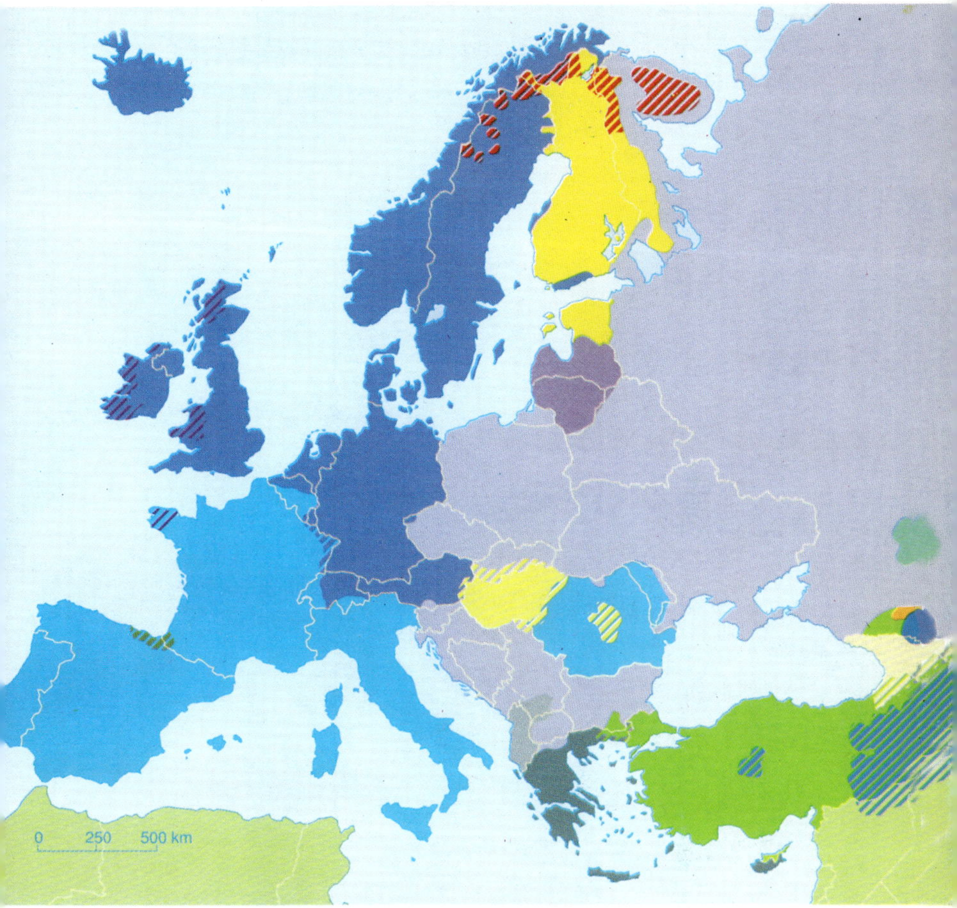

The polyglot continent

he Altaic family

- Turkish group: Karachai, Kazakh, Koumik, Turk
- Isolate: Basque

Hamito-Semitic family

- Semitic group: Arab, Hebrew

Indo-European family

- Baltic group: Latvian, Lithuanian
- Celtic group: Breton, Gaelic, Welsh
- Germanic group: English, German, Danish, Frisian, Flemish, Icelandic, Dutch, Norwegian, Swedish
- Iranian group: Iranian, Kurd
- Roman group: Catalonian, Spanish, French, Friulian, Italian, Ladin, Portuguese, Romansh, Rumanian
- Slav group: Byelorussian, Bulgarian, Macedonian, Polish, Russsian, Serbo-Croatian, Slovakian, Slovene, Czech, Ukrainian
- Isolates: Albanian, Greek

nno-Ugrian family

- Baltic group: Karelian, Estonian, Finnish
- North Laplander group
- North-West Kabardian group
- East Hungarian group
- South Georgian group

EUROPE AND ITS GEOECONOMY: CENTRE AND PERIPHERAL AREA

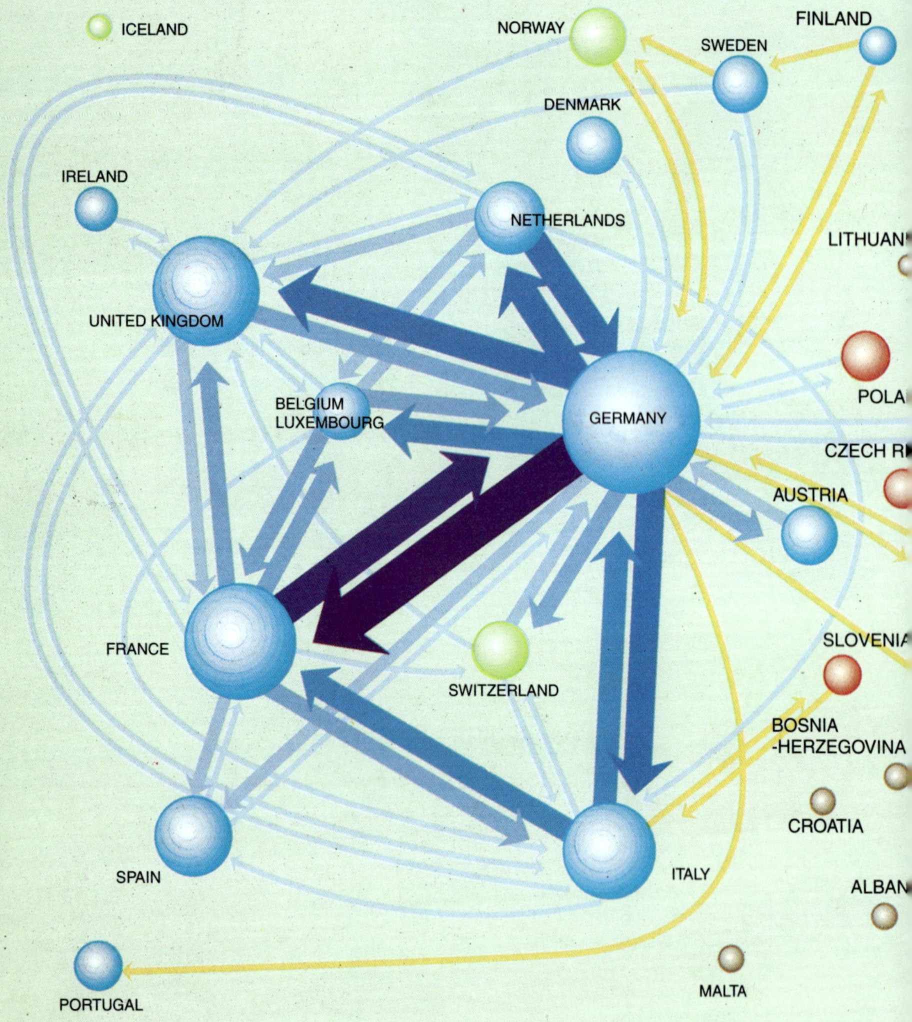

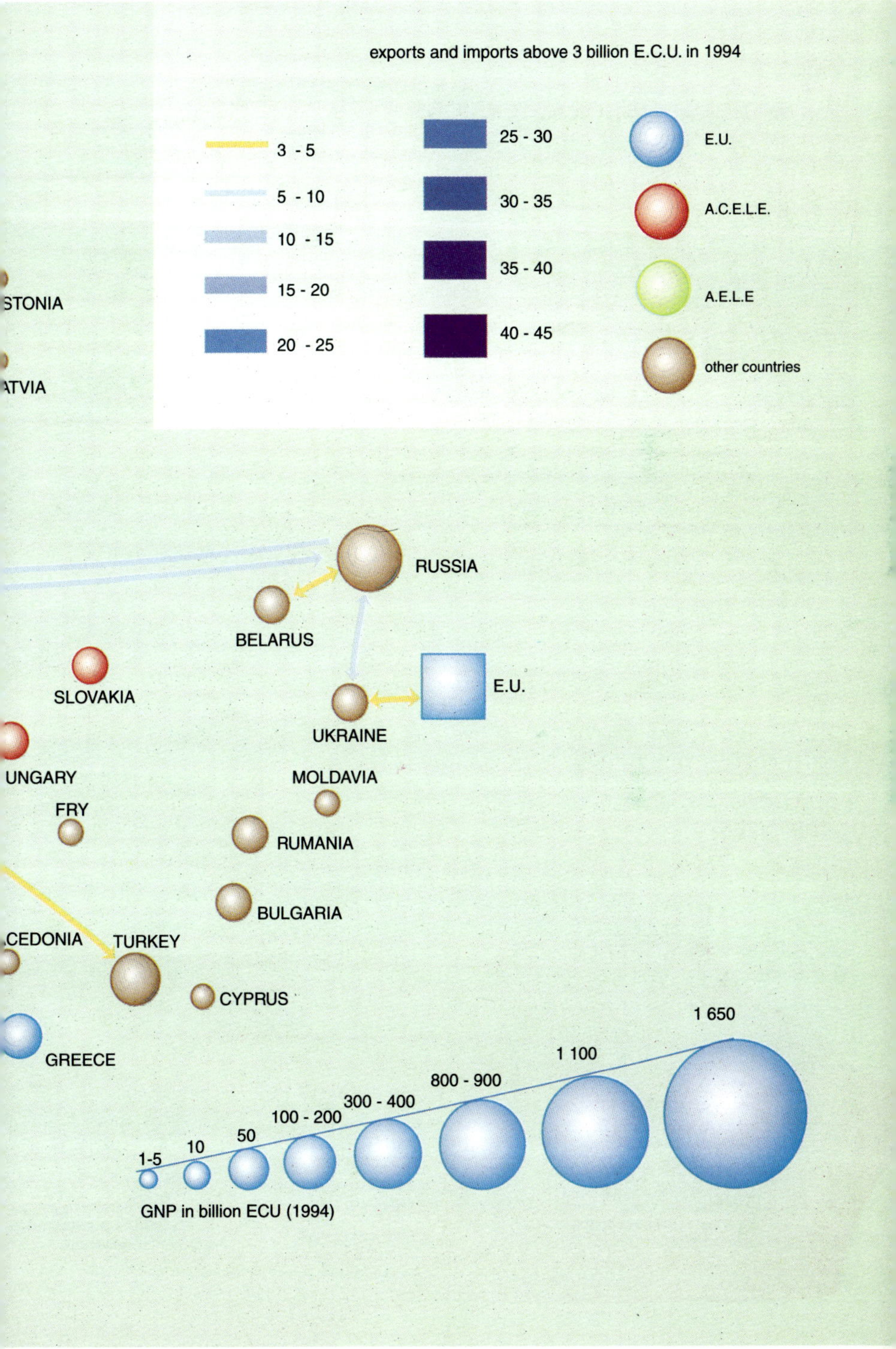

exports and imports above 3 billion E.C.U. in 1994
3 - 5
5 - 10
10 - 15
15 - 20
20 - 25
25 - 30
30 - 35
35 - 40
40 - 45
E.U.
A.C.E.L.E.
A.E.L.E
other countries
STONIA
ATVIA
RUSSIA
BELARUS
SLOVAKIA
E.U.
UKRAINE
UNGARY
MOLDAVIA
FRY
RUMANIA
BULGARIA
CEDONIA
TURKEY
CYPRUS
GREECE
1 650
1 100
800 - 900
300 - 400
100 - 200
50
10
1-5
GNP in billion ECU (1994)

West Europe

- political tensions with violence
- strategies of autonomy
- stakes of social and political integration

Middle and East Europe and its margins

- stakes of reconstruction and democratization
- risk of danger to political status quo
- challenges of modernisation
- stakes of sovereign or of security
- Chechenya
- uncertainty on identity and status

F.N.L. Fünf Neue Länder = five new Länder

old unsettled dispute

borders of Autonomous Republics of Russia

demographic situation modified by wars

main minorities more than 50% of the local population

THE EUROPEAN UNION AND ITS PARTNERS: MIGRATIONS, AID, TRADE

MALTA customs union

borders of Schengen

FRY = FEDERAL REPUBLIC OF YOGOSLOVIA

Common Strategy

PESM (countries that participated in the Euro-Mediterranean, Barcelona 1995, Malta 1997, Marseilles 2000 (except Lebanon and Syria) conferences

European agreements

new Mediterranean agreements

being discussed

EUROPE AND SOME REGIONAL NETWORKS

European Union

INTERREG II Programme

Danube Commission

Baltic Community

Weimar Triangle

Black Sea zone of economic cooperation

Central European initiative

EUROPE FROM THE SECURITY PERSPECTIVE
BETWEEN AMERICAN PROTECTION AND STRATEGIC AUTONOMY

- member of NATO
- 1st phase of enlargement (1999)
- 2nd phase of enlargement? (2002)
- States desiring to enter NATO (2002?)
- partnership for peace
- neutral countries

Headquarters

- NATO
- WEU
- OSCE
- European military Formation

Joint security policy (St-Malo 1998, Cologne 1999, Helsinki 1999)

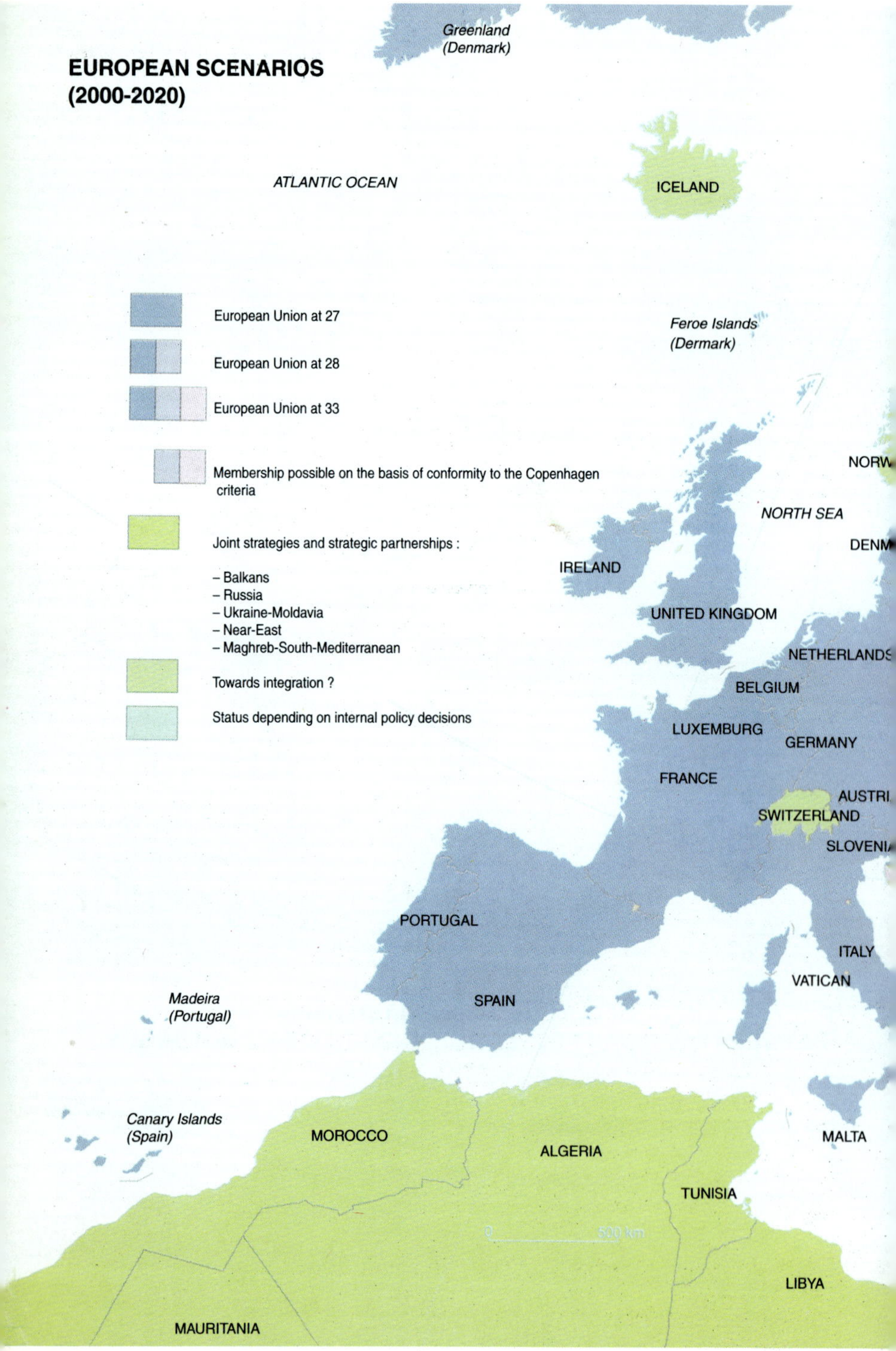
EUROPEAN SCENARIOS
(2000-2020)
European Union at 27
European Union at 28
European Union at 33
Membership possible on the basis of conformity to the Copenhagen criteria
Joint strategies and strategic partnerships :
– Balkans
– Russia
– Ukraine-Moldavia
– Near-East
– Maghreb-South-Mediterranean
Towards integration ?
Status depending on internal policy decisions
Greenland
(Denmark)
ATLANTIC OCEAN
ICELAND
Feroe Islands
(Dermark)
NORTH SEA
IRELAND
UNITED KINGDOM
NETHERLANDS
BELGIUM
LUXEMBURG
GERMANY
FRANCE
SWITZERLAND
SLOVENI
AUSTRI
PORTUGAL
SPAIN
ITALY
VATICAN
Madeira
(Portugal)
Canary Islands
(Spain)
MOROCCO
ALGERIA
TUNISIA
MALTA
LIBYA
MAURITANIA
0
500 km

BARENTS SEA
NORWEGIAN SEA
FINLAND
SWEDEN
ESTONIA
LATVIA
BALTIC SEA
LITHUANIA
RUSSIA
BELARUS
POLAND
KAZAKHSTAN
UZBEKISTAN
ECH REPUBLIC
SLOVAKIA
UKRAINE
MOLDAVIA
HUNGARY
CASPIAN SEA
RUMANIA
CROATIA
TURKMENISTAN
GEORGIA
BLACK SEA
SNIA
RZEGOVENA
AZERBAIJAN
ARMENIA
BULGARIA
YOUGOSLAVIA
MACEDONIA
BANIA
TURKEY
GREECE
IRAN
SYRIA
CYPRUS
IRAQ
LEBANON
MEDITERRANEAN SEA
ISRAEL
KUWAIT
Arab-Persian Gulf
PAL. AUT
BAHRAIN
EGYPT
JORDAN
SAUDI ARABIA
QATAR

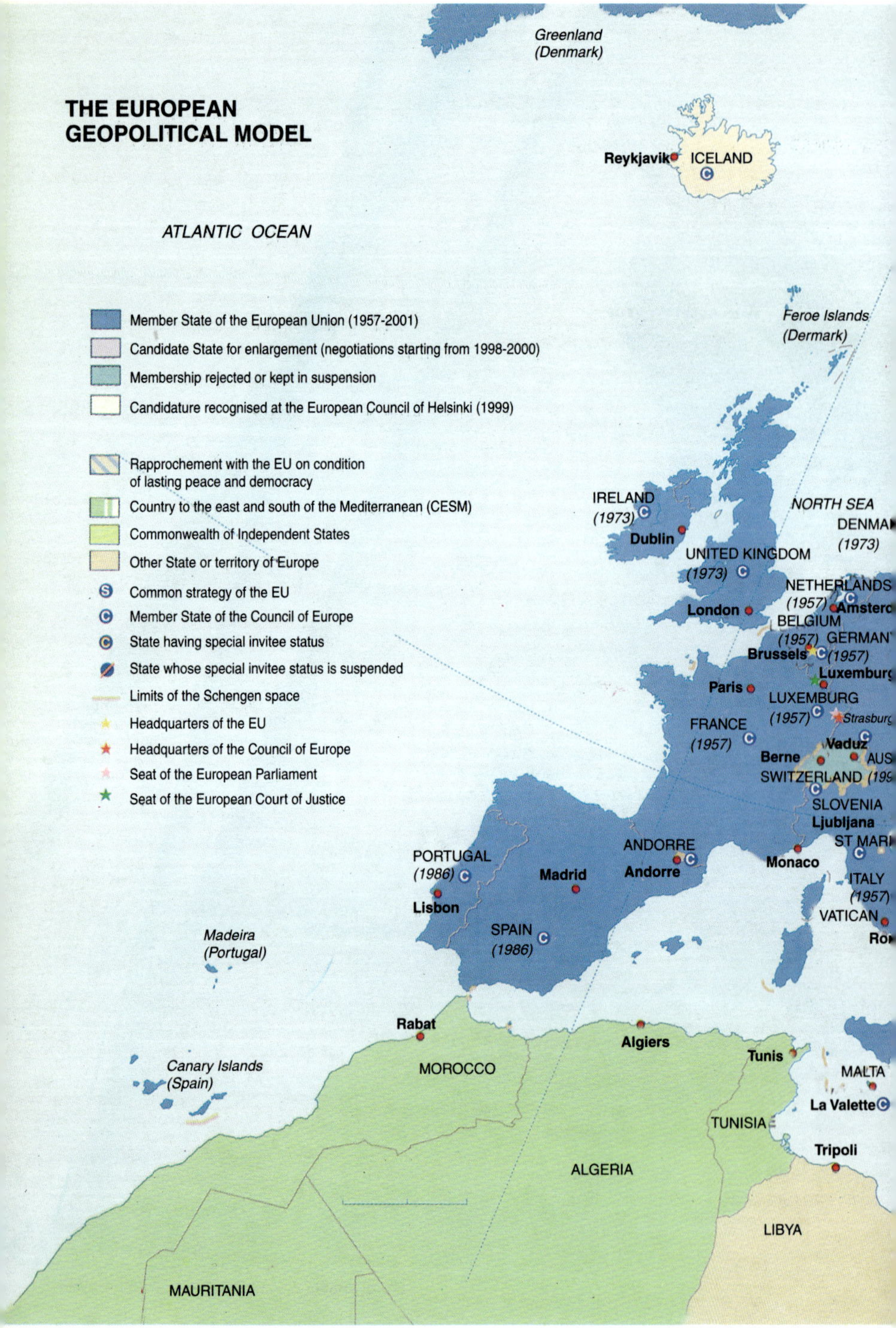
THE EUROPEAN GEOPOLITICAL MODEL
Greenland (Denmark)
Reykjavik
ICELAND
ATLANTIC OCEAN
Member State of the European Union (1957-2001)
Candidate State for enlargement (negotiations starting from 1998-2000)
Membership rejected or kept in suspension
Candidature recognised at the European Council of Helsinki (1999)
Rapprochement with the EU on condition of lasting peace and democracy
Country to the east and south of the Mediterranean (CESM)
Commonwealth of Independent States
Other State or territory of Europe
Common strategy of the EU
Member State of the Council of Europe
State having special invitee status
State whose special invitee status is suspended
Limits of the Schengen space
Headquarters of the EU
Headquarters of the Council of Europe
Seat of the European Parliament
Seat of the European Court of Justice
Feroe Islands (Dermark)
IRELAND (1973)
Dublin
NORTH SEA
UNITED KINGDOM (1973)
London
NETHERLANDS (1957)
BELGIUM (1957)
Brussels
Paris
LUXEMBURG (1957)
Luxemburg
Strasburg
FRANCE (1957)
Vaduz
Berne
SWITZERLAND
SLOVENIA
Ljubljana
Monaco
PORTUGAL (1986)
Lisbon
Madrid
ANDORRE
Andorre
SPAIN (1986)
ITALY (1957)
VATICAN
Madeira (Portugal)
Rabat
MOROCCO
Algiers
Tunis
Canary Islands (Spain)
MALTA
La Valette
TUNISIA
Tripoli
ALGERIA
LIBYA
MAURITANIA

BARENTS SEA
NORWEGIAN SEA
FINLAND
NORWAY
SWEDEN
Oslo (1995)
Helsinki
Stockholm
Tallinn
ESTONIA
BALTIC SEA
LATVIA
Riga
Moscow
Copenhagen
LITHUANIA
Vilnius
RUSSIA
BELARUS
Minsk
KAZAKHSTAN
POLAND
Berlin
Warsaw
Prague
Kiyev
UKRAINE
UZBEKISTAN
CZECH REPUBLIC
Vienna
SLOVAKIA
Bratislava
MOLDAVIA
Kishinev
Budapest
HUNGARY
CASPIAN SEA
CROATIA
Zagreb
RUMANIA
TURKMENISTAN
BOSNIA-HERZEGOVENA
Belgrade
Bucharest
GEORGIA
Bakou
Tblisi
BLACK SEA
AREMENIA
AZERBAIJAN
Sarajevo
BULGARIA
Erevan
YOUGOSLAVIA
Sofia
Skopje
Tirana
ALBANIA
MACEDONIA
Ankara
Tehran
GREECE (1981)
TURKEY
IRAN
Athens
Bagdad
CYPRUS
Nicosia
SYRIA
IRAQ
Beirut
Damas
LEBANON
ISRAEL
MEDITERRANEAN SEA
Tel Aviv
Amman
Kuwait
KUWAIT
Arab-Persian Gulf
PAL. AUT
EGYPT
BAHRAIN
QATAR
Cairo
JORDAN
SAUDI ARABIA

CHAPTER 1

The Power of a Name: Looking at Long Durations

(HISTORIES I)

We other Europeans, we should consider ourselves as travellers who have set sail together on a single ship.

COMENIUS (*Praefatio ad Europeos*, 1645)

I AM giving free rein here to a reflection on the history of European ideas, a retrospective that is necessary since the word 'Europe'—a toponym with variable limits and which are being constantly challenged—preceded the idea, itself carrying changing meanings incessantly being recast. Two pitfalls need to be avoided in the process. Let no one think of this as a new attempt at historical determinism enabling the exhuming from the past of a reality transcending that of Nation-States, to show once again that these gained a victory over an original unity. The moral is evident: Europeans would be well advised to recover, in a surge towards a federation transcending nations, that initial Europe which united them (this was the thesis put forward by Denis de Rougemont, who moreover drew up the first call of the founding Congress which met at the Hague in May 1948). Reflecting on Europe is not akin to searching for a lost paradise, just as Europe, as an organized community, is not historically inevitable. A second pitfall would be to view things only from the perspective of the imaginary, as a drama of perfor-mances, while ignoring the factual truths. Every historical process aims at being not only an investigation into material realities and events, but also into images, ideas and narrations. This dual approach helps in measuring that part of the imaginary which the Europe that we have inherited enfolds; both a sum of more or less firmly established facts, as of the images that have evolved over a period of time.

THE INVENTION OF A TRADITION

Europe, like every depiction with a durable geopolitical purpose, is an invented tradition (in the meaning that Eric Hobsbawn gives it, *The Invention of Tradition*, 1983), in the sense that it serves as an aid to a constructed identity and, should we say, one that is being incessantly refashioned, according to the historical situation of the moment. This geohistorical, and therefore retrospective, view is necessary since, after the 1989 bifurcation, Western Europe has lost the monopoly of the use of the word 'Europe'. While at the time of the formation of the first European Community, during the 1950s, Jean Monnet could say that its borders were fixed by others, by those who felt they should not be part of it, it is now more the contrary situation which prevails. In fact, from Kiev to Ankara, from Nicosia to Tallinn, every nation wants to be a member of the club, and the sooner the better, from their point of view. This is what has brought back into focus the question of the borders of Europe as a whole, a question which had temporarily come to a halt due to the cold war. It induces us, above all, to ponder over its foundations, and hence over the criteria of the geopolitical re-organization currently taking place in the continent. This invention is made of successive strata of interpretations which need to be exhumed.

It is the power of the name 'Europe', legitimate as an enunciation on the imaginary plane, which is coursing through history, since at least five centuries. Other toponyms or geonyms also have the same evocative power. There is notably the word 'America', unduly appropriated by the United States alone, which since long is dominating the discursive panorama of the world. This land presents itself as the antithesis of Europe, a continent of the past, in opposition to the eternal future of a pioneering State with incessantly shifting borders, embodying the West. But their longevity is shorter.

Each era has produced its own depiction of Europe, in terms of a specific conjunction of internal and external factors, and as a response to questionings. It is possible to detect not so much permanencies as reiterations of discourses, in accordance with a helicoidal process which leads to a repetition of the same narrative points. Just one example: the idea that one of the edifices of political Europe is to be found in the precedent of the democracy, albeit restricted, of ancient Athens, is an obvious fact. It is, however, a fairly recent idea, put forward in the middle of the nineteenth century by young democrats fighting for national emancipation. They took hold of the work of George Grote, a British banker, a parliamentarian with a radical outlook and author of a history of Greece (published in 1846), who established that the root of European civilization did not lie in Christianity, but went back to five centuries earlier, in the experiment of Athenians with democracy. He, thus, offered a weapon to democrats who, encouraged by Greek independence against the oppression of the Ottomans, set about opposing the conservative order of the Holy Alliance and an exclusively Christian reading of the idea of Europe. It will be recalled that one of the arguments advanced by the Greek leaders, at the conclusion of the dictatorship of the colonels in the end 1970s, was that the country which had been the cradle of democracy and the propagator of the Tyrian and Cretan myth of Europe could hardly be kept out of the European Community. Thanks to the power of a name they were able to carry conviction and proved more effective in joining the European club than in solving their territorial disputes with Turkey, their adversary. The past takes on a meaning only in terms of its more contemporary utilization. It harbours an inexhaustible storehouse of portrayals and arguments, which can be mobilized, or on the contrary, conveniently forgotten. By way of reminder there is the remark of Ernest Renan on the nation, containing some memorable facts while comprising also a collection of omissions in its common history.

Of the original myth of Europe, one might usefully retain, for contemporary purposes at least, two facts. The first lies in its genesis in the Mediterranean. As we know, there was a tripartite division of the continents, a division of Egyptian origin, and according to Greek mythology, these were referred to by the names of women: Africa, Asia and Europa. As a reminder to living beings, legend extolled these feminine toponyms as being the consorts of gods. While their borders have not ceased to change, do these mythical places owe it to their femininity that they have kept their names since two to three thousand years, to indicate the only too human nature of the cleavages which the gods had wished to sanctify?

According to one of the classical accounts of the origin of the world, Europe was the mother of Minos, king of Crete, a renowned sailor owning a truly powerful naval fleet. Europe, as such, had engendered the oldest amongst the civilizations of the Mediterranean. Ovid has left us a different version in his *Metamorphosis*. According to him, the Phoenician princess was abducted, carried away to Crete and seduced by Zeus, father of the gods. This legend has been painted on Greek vases, on the walls of Pompeii and in the paintings of Titian and Veronese. For the historian Herodotus, this abduction of the daughter of the king of Tyre was only an act of retaliation to avenge the abduction of Io, daughter of the king of Argos, by the Tyrians. History and legend converge to take note of the exchanges of goods and techniques which then took place between the Egypt of the Pharaohs, of which Tyre was a part, and the colonies of ancient Greece. It was while searching for Europe that her brother, Cadmos, conveyed the art of writing to the Greek world. Thus Europe, which etymologists interpret as an Occident, a land of the Western countries as opposed to the Orient, became a Greek geographic concept to denote their new lands to the west of the Aegean Sea, in contrast to their older possessions in Asia Minor. An idea conceived, hence, on the eastern shores of the Mediterranean, just like Christianity.

Europe was, then, a neutral geographic notion. But out of the confrontation between the Greece of antiquity and Persia, over Greece's colonies in the Ionian islands (threatened by the inroads being made by the Persian empire and which called on their motherland to extend security to them), was born a more political meaning. At this time, the European character was described not only in terms of languages (distinct from those of the barbarians, who spoke in words that were barely intelligible, *bar-bar*) and customs, but also of political systems: the opposition between Athenian democracy (albeit very limited) and Persian absolutism.

We note here an astonishing continuity of depiction, seeing that the Persians seem to have been replaced by the Ottomans, then the Turks, in this construction of antagonisms, while Cyprus, in its Greek part, reactivated a strategy of calling on Athens for support.

CHRISTIANITY AND ITS TRANSFERENCE

In this way we see a second characteristic brought out which is distinct to the multiple uses of the word 'Europe', that of a construction through antagonism: on the one side, people aspiring towards freedom, on the other, despotic regimes. This opposition was reactivated in 1789, after that under Napoleon, and naturally between 1945 and 1989, when Western Europe was showcased as being a free bastion against Soviet despotism. The ancient idea that the natural basis of this opposition was to be found in the climatic contrasts (from Hippocrates and Aristotle to Montesquieu), between cold and hot, has remained more enduring than is believed, as can be testified by the discourse on the 'cold' war. In short, the awareness of an external danger and of a structural opposition between an independent continent and foreign empires has fashioned a version of Europe, which can be brought to the fore when circumstances require.

It was, in fact, under the overpowering upsurge of Islam that the primarily Mediterranean Christianity, came to be amalgamated progressively into geographical Europe. But till the fifteenth century, it was referred to more in the context of the Occident and of Christianity. Europe as an idea has given to medieval Christianity a meaning of territorial unity without its having led up to an integrated geopolitical concept. This is due to the schism of 1054 which has durably split up the Christian era: the cleavage has lasted to this day. After 1054, in fact, then the pillage of Constantinople during the fourth crusade, the depictions of the Christianity of reference became confined to its Latin and western facet, with the result that it could not denote a space endowed with a cultural unity. Stemming from a dual confrontation, with Byzantium and with Islam, the idea of Europe remained subordinated to that of Latin Christianity, while coming into rivalry with the attempt at unity of the Germanic Holy Empire of Rome (it was abolished only in 1806). During the crusades, the contenders were called Franks. Some internal elements at unification had a profound influence. There is the role of the Roman Church, its liturgy which provides a common temporal framework; its supreme authority, the Papacy, despite conflicts with the Emperor and the Princes; its uniform territorial organization into dioceses; a common language of the clergy, Latin, the basis of a space of learning; a space of peace with long respites of truce in spite of the wars between Christian sovereigns. These factors contributed towards the structuring of a European socio-cultural space which remained at the same time fragmented into more than five hundred political entities.

The term 'Europeans', which came later into being, is attributed to Pope Pius II (1458–64), a great humanist. After the fall of Byzantium (1453), he made an appeal for a kind of 'joint defence' of the *Respublica christiana* against the Ottomans. In a delayed attempt at the reunification of Christianity he encompassed within it Greece, the area of the Balkans, and Byzantium. The Greek exiles of Byzantium who had taken refuge in the West took part in the establishment of new forms of identification, preparing to replace the term Christianity with the word 'Europe'. Erasmus (1466–1536) himself called on the nations of Europe to unite against the Turks. Boccaccio, in the manner of Dante, had suggested another adjective, *europeico* which could be translated into English by the word 'europic'.

Another contribution of the medieval period, which gives a new turn to the myth of origins, is the image of a centre. The intellectuals of the Middle Ages wanted to give it a meaning. They formulated a principle of history explaining that the development of civilization would spread from the east towards the west, travelling from Greece towards the Occident. They identified a *translatio imperii*, extending from Constantinople and Byzantium towards the Germanic Holy Empire of Rome, and a *translatio studii*, from the Academy of Athens towards Rome, then the University of Paris. This idea of a dual centrality, unified by the presence of Christianity, was an essential stage in the stratification of the depictions of Europe. The big discoveries strengthened this image of centrality by placing the picture of Europe in the centre of the world system. At the same time, with the work of the scholars of the *Respublica litteraria*, who were to be dubbed as 'humanists' by the nineteenth century, Europe became an independent object of discourse, expressing specific cultural values. The book and the map (the Dutch Gerardus Mercator and his modern map of Europe of 1554 in fifteen sheets, then his map of the Euro-centred world; the *Atlas Minor* of Hondius of Amsterdam, 1607, in which the pre-eminence of Europe, assimilated with Christianity, was underlined; the *Thesaurus geographicus* of Abraham Ortelius used the word *Europei* as a synonym of *Christiani*, in 1578) made the contours of the European continent—continuum—more visible and installed a mental map in which Europe was at the core of our projections. But this innovation was accompanied by more metaphorical depictions of Europe. Thus, in some depictions of Sebastian Münster (1588), Europe figured as a queen wearing a crown, in the manner of the Hapsburgs, Hispania shown with a crown on her head, and Bohemia as the heart (this map illustrates the cover of my book, *Fragments d'Europe*, to indicate thereby the ultimately conceivable unity of nations after 1989).

EUROPE IN THIS CENTURY

The idea of Europe, as endowed with attributes of a civilization superior to that of the new world, came progressively to be more accepted, demonstrating less a break with Christianity than an emergence of its secularized version. This was because the Reformation and the religious wars put an end to any show of Christian unity. This fragmentation was theorized by Machiavelli, inventor of the notion of a balance of power between sovereign States. This was a political and not a religious concept, applicable to Europe because of the case of Italian cities at war with Venice. This notion evolved further during the struggle between France and the Hapsburgs and was recast later by Richelieu, inventor of the reason of State. The term is used also in Protestant and Anglo-Dutch circles in the context of the struggle between William of Orange and Louis XIV, placed under the banner of the opposition between 'European liberties' and Christianity (that is to say Catholic). The Reformation eroded the universal Christian order and favoured the setting up of a secular idea of Europe, which prevailed after 1648.

After Richelieu, the search for a balance between princes and nations remained persistently associated with the idea of Europe as a political concept. It was taught as such in the eighteenth century, on the basis of the study of the treatises that the abbot Mably, a diplomat, considered as the archives of European nations (*Le droit public fondé sur les traités*, 1773). Opposed to this realism were the counter-projects of pacifist orientation, from Rousseau (*Projet de paix perpétuelle*, 1756 and 1762; *Jugement sur la paix perpétuelle*, 1756) to Bentham (*A Plan for Universal and Perpetual Peace*, written between 1786 and 1789, published in 1843) and to Kant, the promoter of a 'cosmopolitics' (*Zum ewigen Frieden*, 1795)—successors of Grotius (*De jura belli et pacis*, 1625) and which had their basis in international law. The social contract was devised on the level of nations. Kant innovated by underscoring the fact that peace would last only if the States had republican regimes, that is to say regimes based on the consent of the citizens, notably to take decisions over war.

The eighteenth century ushered in the light of modernity, initiated during the Renaissance and the Reformation, extended by the nationalism and the sense of progress of the subsequent century. For Montesquieu, Europe was a secular idea, associated with freedom, that is to say, free of despotism. The literary and intellectual republic of Voltaire encompassed the sciences. Arts and science took on the dominant position that became the foundation of Europe but not without some contradiction as the Age of Enlightenment was also an age of colonial expansion and of slavery which made their place in the world economy. There arose out of this, a complete separation between Europe and Christianity, while a new polarity set in, the discriminant being the connection with progress. The idea of Europe took on the connotation of a cultural model. But the Republic of Letters disappeared, under the influence of the new linguistic and national barriers, and the cultures of allegiance, which were given the task of a kind of 'border police force'.

EUROPE, AS A HISTORICAL OBJECT

In the era of the end of the century revolutions, the 1776 revolution which led to the creation of the United States, accentuated the autonomy of Europe at the expense of the globalising concept of Occident. The revolution of 1789 can be considered as the embodiment of an idea of Europe identified with a civilized political form of Nation States. As a radical break with the 'Old Regime' and because it occurred in France, the reference nation of eighteenth century Europe, the revolution of 1789 was doubly European in scope. It produced universalist ideas—human rights, political equality, citizenship—which came to grief with Napoleonic imperialism's attempt at political unification imposed by conquest. The project of a universal republic did not succeed in masking during the nineteenth century, the French ambitions for supremacy. The idea of Europe as seen from London, Berlin or Vienna, therefore, remained associated with France; hence its failure.

One of the most important effects of the Revolution was to give a historic dimension to Europe as an object. Europe became a notion subject to the plurality of political interpretations, and correlated to political debates and confrontations. New glimpses were, therefore, cast on the nature and the origin of Europe, whose earlier foundational strata were rediscovered: the triumphant Christianity of the fifteenth century, the notion of the civilization of progress of the eighteenth century and the notion of freedom imported from Greek antiquity. These three strata, separated since long in narratives, came together again and were intensely debated.

The nineteenth century witnessed at least three versions of Europe. There was the re-emergence of a Christian and nostalgic vision of Europe (Chateaubriand or Novalis, Europe or Christianity, 1799)—prolonged by the cult of memory and the taste for museums and cathedrals, which offered to the visitors of the Great Tower, a reminder of Roman Catholic autocracy. Then there was the continent of the Holy Alliance, desirous of restoring the old internal order by the application of the modern strategy of interdependence of States, endorsed by the Congress system, which made it possible to invite Russia to play its counterbalancing role in the concert of Europe. Two novel versions often came in harsh opposition to this. The liberal version was represented by the historian Guizot, who laid stress on the diversity of European civilization and the plurality of political regimes (liberalism against monarchy), aimed at opposing the alliance between throne and altar. A political geography was sketched, demarcating two zones of sociability, those between liberal Europe (of the British model) and conservative monarchies. Saint-Simon, in an address 'to the Parliaments of France and of England' had called for a 'reorganisation of European society', through the formation of a joint Parliament of the two countries, the start of a 'European parliament' (Book III, chapter I). It was formulated in collaboration with Augustin Thierry at the start of the meeting of the Vienna

Congress (summer of 1814: it was sub-titled '*De la nécessité de rassembler les peuples de l'Europe en un seul corps politique, en conservant à chacun sa nationalité*'). The democrats, for their part, who sang the praises of national emancipation, strove to achieve a Europe based, not on the balance of monarchical forces, but on a federation of free nations. These latter made use of the struggle for independence of the Greeks/Hellenics to re-evaluate, as noted earlier, the basis of the idea of Europe, considering it no longer analogous with the Christian religion but rather with the Athenian democracy of antiquity. For European intellectuals, the death of Lord Byron in 1826 marks the date of the vogue for modern nationalist causes.

After 1848, the idea of Europe faded into the background before the reaffirmation of the Nation State, the agent of modernity. Even a Mazzini did not succeed, in spite of his efforts, in situating the (Italian) national aspiration within the ideal of a European unity. If we leave out the anomaly of a Victor Hugo, too much of a precursor and too discordant to be heard, the idea of Europe remained confined to the proclamation of an international law relating to diplomacy, trade and war. Romanticism gave place to political realism; the idea of an affiliation of nations to a higher community was undermined by national rivalries and Bismarck was to declare that '*whoever speaks of Europe is mistaken*'. Nevertheless this period from 1848 to 1914 was, paradoxically, considered as that of the expansion of Europe, assimilated collectively with what appeared to be an unlimited progress. Europe produced on the world, in the age of imperialism, a discourse of material and racial superiority, notably in its confrontation with the East (see Edward Said). It asserted the universality of its values and identified itself with modernity; it constructed the figures of the discourse in comparison to which the other civilizations had to define their identity, like a mirror effect, which is true today for the American hyperpower, capable of establishing terms of reference. The unified identity of Europe wore an imperial face.

The impact of the national interests prevailing from 1914–18, amply justifies the remark by Jean-Baptiste Duroselle that '*between 1914 and 1918, there was no longer a Europe*'. War songs led people in Paris and other cities in the periphery towards the battlefields and the fourteen States of the Berlin Congress became twenty-six after the treaties of Versailles.

THE PROJECT OF EUROPE IN THE ERA OF NATIONALISMS

The paradox of the subsequent period—1919–45—stems from the hiatus between the socio-political and geopolitical realities on the one hand, and the profusion of the projects for Europe on the other hand. The period, 1917–19, marks the intervention of America in the pockets of instability in a Europe incessantly at odds with its past. Out of that and out of the spectacle of the ruins was probably born the insight, already envisioned by Tocqueville (1835), that Europe risked being no more than an 'in-between', a midpoint between the powerful America and the disquieting Russia. Several versions of Europe clashed with each other. The most concrete, and the most creative, was that of the cultural avant-garde flourishing in the metropolises: poetry, literature, theatre, cinema, music, painting, architecture, fashion. Europe became once again a Republic of the arts and of creativity, without borders.

Another version is seen outlined in projects, either of regional emancipation (the new Europe of a Masaryk), or of Austro-Germanic hegemony (the *Mitteleuropa* of Friedrich Naumann), or in ambitious plans for the unity of Europe, in the face of pressures from the extremist Europe of American intent and its encounter with the Russian revolutionary upsurge. The models of 'Paneuropa', mapped by Coudenhove-Kalergi (he excluded the United Kingdom and its vast colonies, as well as Russia) were supplanted by the concrete utopias of a Briand, the first statesman to have formulated the objective of a 'sort of federal link' between States. He was primarily concerned, along with Edouard Herriot, with the relationship between France and Germany. But there was also a third, fascist, version of Europe, which laid stress on the unity of Europe, to be achieved through the destruction of the champions of a cosmopolitan culture (Raul Hillberg and his main writings should be read for this) and the liquidation of the heresy concentrated in Moscow, at the end of a veritable crusade called *Operation Barberousse*, but it failed in front of Stalingrad and Koursk. The Nazi imperial project was also meant to be an attempt at hegemonic unification; it came to a sudden end, its price being paid in tens of millions of lives. In 1998, some, in France particularly, did not give up the desire to bring back to life a fascist *Internationale* which would extend its hold, in the name of Europe.

EUROPE AS AN INNOVATION

The last half a century marks an essential bifurcation in the idea of Europe. Some Europeans attempted, for the first time to institutionalize it by creating a common political framework. The idea, discredited by the tragic regressions of the recent past, had to be reworked, purified, rehabilitated, in order to be established as a utopia, made possible by crumbling nationalisms. This programme for the future was applied in a technical manner, by following a time table, fixing the stages of the integration. But this innovation unfolded in a peculiar geopolitical context since the cold war conferred on Western Europe a more Western than European identity. Europe, perceived by Washington as a source of instability, comprised then the eastern border of 'Euramerica', in direct contact with the Soviet Union and its Central European region. Athens and Ankara belonged to 'Euramerica', Prague, Budapest and Warsaw were in the Eastern bloc.

In accordance with Europe's intellectual tradition, the Europe of the founding fathers was conceived as a community rather than a society, instituting a system of co-operation between Nation-States. Its role as a frontier of the 'Euratlantic' world (a new historical category) prevented it from being raised straightaway to the station of a political society, and the economic field was given preference while an Americanized culture, a binding factor among societies, was spreading. During the cold war, the European identity got structured in dependence, like an in-between, encased within two superpowers with a common destiny which was mutually strengthened by their antagonism. The Europe of Jean Monnet was spirited but subordinate. It was a province of the West.

What has become possible since 1989 is not only this happy 'return to Europe' achieved by the nations of Central and Eastern Europe. It is a matter also, on the plane of the portrayals that we are concerned with here, of a 'return of Europe' replacing the pre-eminent idea of Occident. True, this transition from an all-encompassing idea to the other more familiar one, is only just beginning. But the unification of Germany, accomplished within the dual framework of the European Union and NATO, as a spatial extension of the field of democratic norms towards the centre and the east of the continent and the first negotiations aimed at enlarging the Union confer on the idea of Europe a new significance: that of a principle, organizing the continent on a democratic basis, whatever be its practical institutional modalities. For the countries known as being in transition, Europe is associated both with their break with the Soviet past and, on the positive level, with modernity, inclusive of all the constraints of engineering imposed by the rules of the market and the norms of the Union (as we saw in the new German *Länder* during unification), even if behind it is hidden an idealized American dream nurtured by the diaspora.

The break of 1989 has accentuated the diversity of national cultures (the fourteen States of 1871 had become fifty-four by 1998), which complicates and sometimes paralyses institutions while contributing at the same time towards strengthening the idea of a Europe conceived first of all as a metaphor for organizing our complex civilization. This complexity is evident in the times. The retrospective study of the ideas of Europe has shown the variety and the depth of the strata—some capable of unifying, others of causing disintegration—reminding us that the European project is not an inescapable one. In the last half a century, nations have involved themselves in a great effort to institutionalize the idea into a form of community, thus conferring on Europe a constructed identity. The players in this effort have been, and continue to be, the Nation-States concerned over their interests so that the relationship between the idea of an organized Europe and the national idea does not work in reality like an antagonistic couple, but constitutes the two elements of an interaction aimed at structuring an edifice.

In the contrary event, it would not be possible to understand why France, one of the oldest Nation-States of Europe, should have so deeply involved itself in giving concrete shape to a modern idea of Europe, as a system of co-operation, in its full meaning. This is so, also for Germany before, during and after its reunification. Europe is the outcome of a strategy of discourse of the European Nation-States, essential centres of Europe in the making, which see in it the modalities of their coexistence. The fact remains that the nationalist drift, populism, the self-perversion of values and the propensity that too many Europeans have for forms of inquisition are, as Hans Kohn underlines, '*Europe's inner devils*' (*The Twentieth Century*, 1949), the major threat weighing on the plans for unity: '*Twentieth century man has been witness to and has experienced the diabolical powers of history. What seemed to have belonged to the past has reappeared: fanatic faith, leaders who consider themselves infallible, slavery and massacres, the uprooting of entire populations, pitiless barbarism*'. That is why it is not enough to seek to reassure oneself by bringing to mind the common origins of Europeanity in the extended Middle Ages (from the end of Antiquity to the French Revolution, according to Le Goff). It is important, above all, as Habermas underlines (*Praxis International*, 1992), to create political confidence in the role that Europe is to play in the new century.

CHAPTER 2

The Outlook, for Europe

(HISTORIES II)

To unity, culture always says yes;
economics more or less yes;
politics remains reticent.

FERNAND BRAUDEL (*Grammaire des civilisations*,
Belin, 1963, Flammarion, 1987)

EUROPE is neither inevitable nor does it exist from time immemorial. It will not necessarily come into being sooner or later. It will simply be the product of time. There is no historical determinism to it and several futures are possible/impossible, probable/improbable. These are made of segments of the logic of evolution and of two irrationals, chance and the leeway provided by human freedom, as by human will.

The Europe of material realities is the other side of our history. To understand Europe is to accept straightaway the dialectics of convergence and divergence, to make good use of it and to admit that while Europe does not come within the purview of teleology, it may be perceived as being a process. It is not the end that counts but time, the driving force of conceivable projections.

What use would be served, *hic et nunc*, by a reflection on the historical convergence in Europe when the trend today is towards preparing for the immediate future: towards a single currency, enlargement, foreign policy and joint security and to the management of crises in the peripheral areas averse to democratic practices? The reason for the existence of the project for European unity would no longer need to be demonstrated, even less debated publicly because, from the era of Jean Monnet and Jacques Delors, it is the time schedule of meetings and councils, marked by date limits which naturally are adhered to, which has replaced a programme. The national politicians in charge and the European administrators have made themselves past masters of the art of clockwork precision and this ability to control collective time suffices to legitimize their decisions. The sense of perspective has been lost and with it the meaning of the common effort required from citizens, who have hardly been called upon, by the decisive political elites. But this seems to matter little provided the community clock turns constantly.

THE FAMILY CLOCK

Till now, the discourse on the past of Europe has served a dual purpose. For one, by invoking the barbaric deeds of the century, it has been necessary to show that the reason behind the construction of Europe was to set up a peace between nations historically antagonistic to each other and hereafter reconciled within a common project. We see there again the origins of the federalist dream whose supporters have always thought of the Nation-State as a transitory from of European culture, fallen from grace due to the conflicts and wars engendered by pride in its exclusivity. This approach is today reaching its limits as seen in the unexpected resistance of nations, the encompassing nations and the nations within the States of the European Union. Even if the strategists who formulate German policy may deny it, it is indeed in the name of the nation that German unity was forged. In France, where the present Union was mostly shaped, the idea of nation is deep-seated even if some time is required before the two rungs of the ladder of sovereignty: State and Union, complement each other, the second enabling the first to get its voice heard in the competition reigning in the world, and finally strengthening it. The Union is the original framework of a renewed immutability of nations, without dominant nationalisms. Decisions are arrived at by the European Council, bringing together the elected leaders of each nation, heads of State and of governments and their ministers. The original hypothesis of the federalist radicals has hence not been concretized. They had undoubtedly underestimated, in their re-reading of European history, the central role of the long spells of national formation.

Or then, in a process which, this time, is positive, the past of Europe has been re-examined, re-read in a near eschatological perspective in order to search within it for the legitimization of the rhetoric of an association and the moral foundations of the will for a unitary set-up. The European past is excavated in the manner of the archaeologist who digs out the proofs of the glorious existence of a city of antiquity which has harboured an ideal society. Of this past, only the premises relevant to the present work will be examined, only the precursory signs of a unity within reach will be selected, which have proved the founding fathers of 1945–57 right. They are sorely missed today for they could have illumined the path. The European Union is already more than forty years old. At this age, does one still need a father?

These two approaches have largely exhausted their effects. The dream of absolute federalism does not hold in the face of the interrogation over national identities and over the heterogeneity of regional expressions. With the return of the Balkanic conflicts, with interrogations over the future of the other Europe, the aggressive thrusts of Anglo-Saxon liberalism and the tyranny of the short term, since only the event that has been publicized has a market value, the process of a purposeful action, resting on an optimistic re-reading of the history of Europe, has reached its limits. Yet, the very word 'convergence' belongs now to official vocabulary, even in its least attractive aspect. This is because, being subject to the famous criterion of statistics, it is the one that lends itself most to computation. Since the Maastricht, Treaty (1992) the word 'Union' has replaced what was the more appropriate, because more realistic, concept of 'Community'.

This telescoping of the times complicates the reflection on Europe as an object. 'While a history that is close at hand is rushing rapidly towards us, a history of the distant past is accompanying us at a slow pace'. This dialectics of the moment and of duration, has been devised as a method of study of civilizations by the historian Fernand Braudel. Getting summarized sometimes in the astounding impact of events which are more visible than intelligible and of growing but invisible mutations, it illumines the comprehension of Europe, understood here precisely as a phenomenon of historical convergence. Or rather as a discourse and an attempt at convergence.

The word 'Europe' is fortunately polysemous and, depending on the speaker, it may signify hope or constraint, utopia or failure. Many meanings are possible. Drawing on the sources of geography, it could mean a continent without fixed borders; on those of culture, it would be heir to the *Respublica litterarum* and the Age of Enlightenment; from the viewpoint of history, the centuries of struggles between nations and empires; from that of economy, the necessity for an open or a closed market; from that of law, the guarantee of freedom of the individual and of his pre-eminence over the group. The correlatives of Europe are frequently terms connoting union, for whatever duration. Among these the unity that the different Christianities dream of: economic integration, the due process of superior European law, the identity of political models, a common law, a voluntary alliance of nations, a federation of States, a Union of member States signatories to founder treaties, a common policy, the criteria of budgetary and financial convergence.

Everything is happening as if, over long as well as over short durations of time, Europe has been a socio-political configuration, inseparable from a project whose objective is close to that of fusion, a collective figure of the wider family seeking tirelessly to come together and maintain the mythical harmony of a golden age. The metaphor of the construction of the house of Europe, reminds us insistently of the potency of this fantasy of the family. Is it not finally the happiness of citizens which dictates what today is the unprofessed objective of any democratic political discourse? Moreover, the State and governments have placed themselves at the service of the individuals who aspire to this happiness. The day before yesterday, it was meant to ensure the glory of nations and the expansion of territories. Yesterday, with the help of decades of prosperity, it by way of Europe, had to provide—the original meaning of the word 'providence'—for the welfare of all. Today the project has not changed and it has to strive to achieve a wide symmetry and avoid the excessive social disparities engendered by economic competition.

In the intellectual sluggishness reigning in Europe and in the face of the political crisis which is foreshadowed, if the mechanisms of decision designed for the six founder nations are not rapidly modified, it is necessary to break with the classical process seeking in the past that which unites so as to more easily discard that which divides. It is proper in the present event to reverse the approach, by placing oneself both in the present, in order to truly innovate and set out the principles of a new convergence through a wide and continuous public debate, as well as in the past, in order to rework the divergences and regain a perspective. We should conceive of today's Europe on the basis of its past, not in order to legitimize a project of unity which on the whole is a fairly recent one, but in order to take a long duration view of that which specifies Europeanity, an original European identity, alongside that of other worlds.

THE EUROPEAN COMPLEX

While a re-reading of the European past aimed at the quest for an inescapable progression towards unity was necessary at the initial stages of European construction following the national and ideological conflicts of the first half of the century, this process is no longer justified. Because it does not enable us to understand the original disjoining that the contemporary project at unity constitutes. And because a determinist vision forecloses any debate on whatever divides, and prevents us from understanding why the political unity of tomorrow, much vaunted in treaties, remains a difficult, if not an inaccessible objective.

The idea is, therefore, not that a historical convergence be contemplated as a process which has in a way been finalized, liable to undergo a near theological interpretation. This is reminiscent of the eternal project of the unity of Christians around the Papacy, the ultimate objective of the geopolicy of the Vatican on the continent and in the Near East. To this eschatological reading, we may prefer a study of the cumbersome tendencies of European societies to underline the parallelism of trajectories, which does not imply an identity of forms, practices and successful culminations.

In this spirit, Europe can be conceived of as a 'complex', a network that has been woven together. Like the warp and woof of a colourful tapestry, the Europe contemplated in the long term presents a combination of basic elements which, by themselves, do not in any way induce a unity in ways of behaviour. Less importance is given by this means to conflicts and tensions, the manifest signs of continuous differences, than to the objective factors of convergence, to facts relating to structure, so as to specify the mental outlook of Europeans considered as a distinct historical category. This approach, even though partial but which can open up a whole range of discussion, underlines the eminent place occupied by very ancient though slow to spread, structures of commonality across European space.

The historical approach has brought out the original traits of the complex (the multisecular fight against Islam—Saint-Jacques-de-Compostelle invented an extreme Western replica of Mecca). Once external security was more or less assured, a stubborn development was noted of specific liberties, of franchises, of group privileges clashing and battling each other in the countryside, then in the cities. In the name of liberties, the States were inventing the reason of State as the *ultima ratio* and breaking the earlier and, for a long time, structuring unity of Christianity. It was by pricking the bubble of this first basis that the national States emerged, and with them, humanism, free will and science. The dialectics of the fragmentation of Europe into States which followed matching principles but confronted each other during wars in order to add on to their heritage and vie with each other in prestige, was very much in place and had not subsequently ceased to operate. A convergence was to be perceived in the aspirations of nations to free themselves of empires, whether the encompassing adversary be the Germanic Holy Roman Empire for France or, much later, Soviet Union for Ukraine. The notion of a more individual liberty was becoming clearer, from the Renaissance to the Reformation, from the French Revolution to the triumph of liberalism and rationalism. True, a common reservoir did subsist and Europe was criss-crossed by these philosophical or political currents of thought. To give an example, the Metternich System established a concert of nations based on a coalition of monarchies opposed to the progression of republican currents and to movements for national emancipation. Nothing in all that produced any 'unity', but these enlightened despots derived their thinking from common references.

A more socio-historical perspective specifies the elements of the basic European complex, valid, truly speaking, above all for Western and Central Europe, as the areas of Ottoman occupation and Byzantian influence which had somewhat lagged behind in their evolution. The elements constituting this societal complex would be the following ones (if we follow the work of Henri Mendras concerning Western Europe, 1997). What stands out first of all is the primacy of the individual over the social group, the latter being at the service of the former which derived its legitimacy from evangelical individualism. This was despite the desire of the Church, the guardian of the understanding of Biblical texts, and with the support of the Reformation and of Roman law, from the time of Justinian to Napoleon, to act as a mediator. The Age of Enlightenment perfected this ideological innovation since it was the individual, as a citizen, who laid down the basis of the national will, on condition that a good government ensure his happiness. Then there was the invention of the nation, another European innovation, which won recognition during the course of the centuries against imperialism, its latest manifestations being of the Soviet and the Serb variety. The nation was born out of stable peasant spaces and had a configuration in which were found together a soil, a language and a people, separated from the others by borders as limited as the patch of meadow belonging to the peasant. While the empire was multiple, a gathering together of communities, the nation was a single entity and had its basis in the consent of free citizens. Then, towards the sixteenth century, probably connected with the doctrine of the separation between the temporal and the spiritual, between politics and religion, the State and the Church, and with the effects increased tenfold by scientific innovations, the sense of progress and the industry of the cities, capitalism was born and seen to spread. Finally, the big innovation lay in the application of the law of government by the majority. The rights of the minority—half less one—were guaranteed by 'The Rule of Law', since all citizens are free and equal before the law.

This common trunk, reconstituted in its main features to throw light on the present, in no way does away with the diversity of the family-style structures, of the types of capitalism, religious beliefs, political practices, of the concrete modes of organization of the State, the criteria for national affiliation, social hierarchies, or value systems or behaviours in the face of birth or death. All these are endless material for the comparative analysis of the tastes and proclivities of Europeans. The greater the advances made by historical knowledge and statistics, better the diversity of societies was grasped. In the explanation of historical convergencies, the reality of this common matrix of a socio-historical nature, distinguishing Europeans from other centres of civilization, was therefore formulated as a first hypothesis.

The second hypothesis, a sociological one, stems from an acceleration of the phenomena of convergence in the last half a century as regards the nations of Western and Central Europe which have been prey to parallel mutations. They have witnessed rapid economic growth and technical mutations modifying their social systems, an end to the dominant role of the peasantries and to a patrimonial concept of the nation, comparable demographic modifications (lengthening of life expectancy, ageing, lowering of fertility), a reversal of the relations between the individual and social groups (families, organizations, parties) to the advantage of the former (who must determine his own values and fit himself into the networks). Cultural relativism has spread, succeeding the sentiment that each nation is an exception, a common quest for aesthetic or eschatological references (the travels of the Pope) and, paradoxically, an avowal of the variety of societies. According to Mendras, 'by enriching itself, Western society has become more flexible, the different elements of society have acquired a greater degree of freedom with relation to each other. The growing complexity of the systems of relationships between sectors, between players, between institutions restores a flexibility to the whole of society: civil society places itself in between political society and economic society'.

On the whole, two types of historical convergence fit into each other. Over the long term, there is the slow spread in Europe of common referents, including national and politico-religious conflicts since they are as much its expression as its driving force. In the post-war era, under the major effect of transformations on the economic plane (growth as a powerful factor of integration) and the geopolitical plane (the external constraint of a concurrent Marxist ideology), there is a deliberate coming together with a view to achieve a cohabitation of the nations of Western Europe, under the protection of an external Europe, a North American Europe.

THE THREE UNITIES OF EUROPE

Another peculiarity of the Europeans in the world is their attachment to the rhetorics of unity. We find undoubtedly in Latin America, an offspring of Europe, a kindred aspiration since the time of Bolivar, a more conquest-oriented objective in the Islamic lands, and the constant search for unity by India as a State-civilization. Similarly, the objective of unity has not ceased to haunt the elites of China and permeates singularly their contemporary diplomacy. To keep the unification of several States as a political objective, in accordance with a process of deliberate convergence, is a fairly recent idea on the scale of European history even if some utopian notions were indeed formulated in earlier times, as we know, by the Republic of Letters.

The change that occurred in the middle of the twentieth century was that of the emergence of an explicitly European awareness. In his *Discours à la nation européenne* written in 1933, Julien Benda noted the role of the big movements that had spanned the history of the continent: the crusades, the Reformation, revolutions, the spingtimes of peoples, colonizations and the class struggles, and he said in conclusion: 'all these European movements did strictly nothing for the unity of Europe. Why? Because Europe, while conducting them, did not become aware of them as Europeans; because its people were living through a commonality of interests, they were experiencing an identity of sentiments, but were not consciously aware of it.'

The post-war decisions—the Hague Congress of 1948, the 1949–52 Marshall Plan, the 1949 Council of Europe, the ECCS of 1951 which marks the first concrete blow struck at sovereignty, the six-nation Treaty of Rome of 1957—instituted a historical rent, opening a breach between the real-life Europe and the Europe of design and thought. But limits appeared quickly since: 'Europe will not come into being at a single stroke, nor by an overall construction: it will be made through concrete achievements, setting up first of all a real solidarity'. The project retained had its basis in one element: the economy. The road through politics initially reached a dead end, the Council of Europe having failed to become a melting pot on account of the British opposition, followed by the rejection by French parliamentarians (1954) of the Community for Defence. The result was that German rearmament took place within an Atlantic framework dominated by the United States. In 1957, as in 1986 (Single Act), it was convergence through the economy which was chosen. It was not till 1992 that convergence through politics was set out in the treaty, but this clause was not applied while the monetary union aspect became the exclusive preoccupation of European players. At this stage, the Union was not a union; what existed was a large market and also a 'community of law' to quote the expression used by Walter Hallstein, the first President of the Commission, since rules, directives and decisions prevailed over the internal law of the nation.

If we put this breach back into perspective, we cannot but bring to mind the analysis of Braudel on the unities of Europe. As he recalls in his *Grammaire des Civilizations*—a work significantly broken up into two parts, Europe and non-Europe—there are a multiplicity of possible bases for the processes of unification, art and intellect, economics and politics: 'To unity, culture always says yes; economics more or less yes; politics remains reticent'.

The brilliant unities of art and intellect 'meetings, harmonies, give to European civilization an almost uniform appearance, as if it was pervaded by one and the same light'. Philosophies, for their part, are also messages of unity, while objective science is strictly single, from the moment of its first conquest. Thus, European space forms a cultural field that is fairly coherent and has since long asserted its presence.

The more solid unities of the economy—today the large domestic market, surmised to be the guarantor of the modernized welfare State—are not an innovation since Europe has long since found itself entangled in the mesh of a unitary style economy, organized around authoritarian and preferential centres. It formed at a very early date a coherent space on the material plane and the convergence in this field has been quite clearly established, all the more so as it rests on interests that are intertwined (60 per cent of its trade is between members of the Community).

But even so, the sweep of the Maastricht Treaty extends beyond the sole material dimension. The monetary union partly eludes the rationality of economics considering that the debate on the stability and the strength of the Euro is in consonance with the acknowledged and considered question of a 'good currency'. Everyone dreams of a stable currency, having its own intrinsic value independent of the interplays of exchange. But since, in order to become a variable in this interplay it has to be recognized on the political level by public opinion, it plays a symbolic role. It is a proof of the ability of the authorities to control the workings of the social order. As it is on the question of a common currency, confidence can come only from the existence of a European political order, wielded by an authority capable of asserting its presence. The single currency is finally more in line with the formation of a political order of which it is a modality, than with the integration of markets and the end status of the monetary authority of Frankfurt. Being a sign of the strength of political institutions in the face of civil society, it expresses the appreciation that the players hold for the credibility of the European political project, a new gold standard engraved in an intangible bronze.

One may, thereafter, wonder at the uncertain unities on the political plane that have marked the last half a century. The great similarity in political regimes has been further substantiated by the success of the transitions to democracy that have taken place in Central and Eastern Europe and the progressive extension of the due process of law. In spite of these, it is the reversal of the federalist project, the divergent visions of Europe, the disappointments engendered by the timidity of common policies, that have thrown the burden of their weight into the matter of the supposed 'impotence' of Europe.

These political hazards are not new in a continent which, as Helmut Kohl recalls, has experienced a war every forty years since the last thousand years. While States are engaged since several centuries in the same game of political rivalry, one of whose constants has been to check the attempts at hegemony by a single one of them, history has been interspersed by the struggle of nations against those who laid claim to the Empire. Even very recently, it is learnt that one of the preoccupations of German diplomacy has been to prevent the formation of a coalition of States concerned over the effects of power arising out of unification. France supported Rumania in NATO and it is urging Cyprus, a client country of Greece in the Mediterranean, to avoid an enlargement of the Union restricted to Central Europe, perceived in France, partly mistakenly, as a zone of exclusively German influence.

From this point of view, the European Union is partially participating in a game of balance of power, hence the increased standing being granted to the 'small' States (Belgium, Luxembourg for instance, where many of the institutions of the Community are located). The British strategy with regard to the 'continent' is steadfast on this matter. The British Prime Minister, Tony Blair has chosen the path of entry in preference to the paralysing abstention of his predecessor.

Even if the lesson has been learnt that a single State cannot grab hold of the house of Europe by force, precluding the game of violent unities, even if Europe as a project has served as a factor of pacification, it is not certain that Europeans have given up the game of the 'European balance', of the 'concert of nations', and of the 'balance of power' so clearly analysed by Kissinger, which marked the start of the modern diplomatic practices stemming out of Richelieu's invention of the 'reason of State'. Today, the strongest State has to offer pledges of integration and behave as a 'useful power'. Failing this, it will be like an empire without an emperor, devoid of political coherence, the Europeans having failed in the invention of a 'reason for Europe' acceptable to the rest.

This shows to what extent the Community remains based on national realities and is, therefore, traversed by widely divergent 'visions of Europe' whenever the question arises of safeguarding or promoting the specific interests of its member States. The inescapable role of these visions has moreover been analyzed (Michel Foucher and Ignacio Oyarzabal, *Visions of Europe*, 1995) and contributes towards explaining the impossibility of adopting joint external policies. While bringing differences out into the open is a part of the diplomatic process, it is rare for it to invade the public arena. In fact, it is not enough for the Community to attend to the matter of bringing civility into the relations between States. It is important also that it should forge joint endeavours in the required fields, to maintain order at the periphery and to enhance its credibility. This leads to the question of power which tends more to shock a number of societies of the continent than to conjure dreams. It also fashions new rifts between States and between their leaders and societies. Even if a joint external policy is demonstrated, only a minority of States has conserved the idea of a politics of power. This could however be contemplated as being a condition for the maintenance of the European identity and as a factor for peace and equilibrium.

THE PARADOXES OF CONVERGENCE OR OF THE PROPER UTILIZATION OF DIVERGENCIES

The principle of the three unities does not, therefore, fully enter into play. Yet, 1989 could have been the starting point for a new impetus to the processes of convergence. Indeed, the picture sketched earlier is complemented by several unprecedented facts. Europe is no longer divided into enemy nations as in the past. The classical ideological conflicts seem to have been left behind with the spread in European space, of democratic practices. The European Union has survived the end of the cold war which had witnessed its birth and, as is being unwisely stated, the number of members of this reorganized group is destined to double. Finally, the non-Europe of Braudel is becoming a factor incessantly more present in the process of intra-European convergence (globalization, migrations, security, images, will to intervene in distant crises). These mutations lead to the challenging of the pre-eminence of nations as being the triple framework for economic activities, for the political process and for cultural life. Will Europe then find its salvation in a post-national convergence? It is not as simple as all that.

The nation, a European invention, remains at the core of every European geopolitical process. The most remarkable feature of the history of the continent, over several centuries, partakes of a dual movement: on the one hand, the joining together of kingdoms, principalities, entities and cities to form larger political units under the authority of the State, whose sovereign seeks to extend his 'domain'. On the other hand, as seen more recently, there is the metamorphosis of empires encompassing diversified communities, breaking up into several separate nations through an assertion of the national will. Thus, since 1989, around twenty new States have put in an appearance on the map of Europe, in the place of more or less voluntary federations. Some, witness the case of the Ukraine or Croatia, are decidedly nations late in the coming, as were Germany and Italy in times gone by. Others, such as Byelorussia or Moldavia, are still searching for an identity. Nonetheless, this does not prevent these States, once formed and having achieved their sovereignty, from presenting their candidature for membership of the Council of Europe, and a good half of them, of the European Union.

Thus, the people of Europe are driven by a permanent tension between the assertion of their diversity, of their singularity, of a narcissism over small differences and the manifest quest for an impossible unity. This phenomenon of fragmentation has been analyzed elsewhere, to define Europe as an intentional process for the bringing together of national fragments: a community 'containing' a field of forces (see *Fragments d'Europe*). This explains the permanence of the visions and of the national and divergent geopolitical portrayals.

There is more. Within the framework even of the Union, the 'inner nations', from Scotland to the Basque country, are raising their voices, and are on the way to obtaining or to consolidating, at variable speeds, the attributes of sovereignty that they claim. Even in the centralizing United Kingdom, devolution of power is the order of the day for Scotland and more partially for Wales. The insertion of these nations within a multi-State European unit appears as a factor for harmonizing the relations between the inner nations and the central authority. Conversely, in Germany, a federalist country, the rivalries of influence are growing between the southern *Länder* (led by Bavaria which refuses to forget its status of *Freistaat Bayern*) and the Federation, accused by the former of enhancing its powers by the very fact of the intergovernmental nature of European construction.

Finally, contrary to the European federalist dreams, the 'nation' puts up a greater resistance than foreseen to the phenomena of integration and of free exchange. This is seen in countries ranging from Denmark to France, and etched in between, in Norway, a State independent since only a century. The oldest nations are sometimes more reticent about the devolution of sovereignty—witness the debates in France and in the United Kingdom where European construction is sometimes accused of destroying the very idea of nation. But the reverse processes are noted in Spain and Portugal where high hopes for Europe have come in tandem with the transition to democracy.

All in all, a paradoxical convergence is observed in Europe since each people has followed the same trajectory, that of the promotion of its own sovereignty—in a movement which is reminiscent of and sometimes an extension of the negotiations of the Communes of the Renaissance—to obtain the guarantee written in their charters of freedom and their franchises. Convergence, seen this time from a geopolitical angle, would result from the parallel advance of these long-term processes. They have not come to fruition, ending up in an increased but viable diversity if they are inscribed in a widened and contractual framework. From this point of view, it is the function of the European Community to cultivate the relationships between States by channelizing the power equations. That again is another innovation, that of an original geopolitical system of an interaction made peaceful between kindred nations, in accordance with a novel mode of management of dissimilarities.

Thus, therefore, all along this central axis of history, some lasting trends have emerged. On the one hand, Europeans have crossed over from a geopolitics of closed societies, structured in accordance with the antagonistic friend/enemy configuration and therefore a game leading nowhere, to a geopolitics of open societies, marked by the interdependence of States and the pronounced role of the play of power at different levels. The very notion of national interests is partly called into question to give place to that of shared interests, at least in the West European space. Moreover, the nation remains the basic political and cultural framework and the notable place of residence of the citizen. One of the reasons for this is language, the vector of the circulation of ideas between the upper and the lower echelons of society and, via the debate in the national public space thus verbalized, the tool for the emergence of the idea of a political community. Language is a central edifice in political awareness and in the diverse nature of the European fragments.

The European process itself introduces breaches, for example there is the gap between the nation as a territory of activity, and the real geoeconomic space. Similarly, alliances get forged between the national elites which, through their intersecting legitimations (a little like the intersecting interests of enterprises) seek to emancipate themselves from the democratic delegation which gave a basis to their legitimacy. The European administration is making advances and under its patronage Europe is becoming an assembly of integrated States, or at least interlinked States. The production of norms and of the rule of law is forming the framework of societies, but they can hardly discuss these aspects; there is not yet a public European space. Finally, as a corollary to what has been noted earlier, the administered Europe is not a political project with which the citizen can identify himself; and the nation ceases to be a place of debate the moment decisions are arrived at in another, supranational framework. If, moreover, the nation no longer shoulders its republican role of civic integration, it becomes an under-utilized framework, in short an 'idle nation', as Paul Thibault has pointed out.

We return, hence, to the complex, the space for interaction between the forces of unity—the market, common values, shared interests, the will to break with the past of conflicts, the aspiration for a new, cosy Welfare State—and the factors of dissociation. These contradictions, which form, nevertheless, the basis of any somewhat deliberately premeditated undertaking, are all the more easily expressed, as European thought is, in its very method, the offspring of doubt. Historians speak rather of the critical mind. Philosophers, heirs to René Descartes, lay stress on doubt, which, true, needs to be removed to give place to certainty and which is the harbinger also of the modern scientific approach. Unless doubt be only the final ruse of a good conscience.

OF THE PROPER UTILIZATION OF DOUBT

It has been written in the introduction that Europe, a province of the world, is primarily a continent of doubt and of criticism. These philosophic notions describe not only the mind of the Europeans (attached to the primacy of the individual and to the freedom of action and judgement) but also their geography and their practice, uniting an extreme and continuously asserted variety (of landscapes, languages, nations and peoples, historical trajectories, cultures and visions) with a rhetoric of union (the quest for the unity of national States and sometimes of peoples who have been split, an increased convergence of economic practices, an extension of democratic processes). Doubt prevails everywhere and pervades the public discourse to the point sometimes of summarizing and exhausting debate on it.

Doubt exists over Europe itself, which actually may never have existed, an option explored in earlier paragraphs. Doubts over this unit reactivated themselves on the geopolitical limits, with uncertain and shifting borders. Europe is seen as a territorial unit made up of more than around fifty ancient or more recent States and around sixty nations or ethno-linguistic entities imbued with a calling for or an aspiration towards nationhood. From this point of view, the integration and the coming into being of the European community are complicating the depictions of Europe by dissociating the fifteen member States from the non-member countries aspiring to join them. The difficulty increases when we invoke the word 'Europe', while alluding to the deliberate construction of a durable association between around fifteen States and nations which, with the signing of the Treaty of Maastricht (1992), made the strategic choice of becoming a part of the European Union (see Chapters 4 and 5).

Doubt also exists over the identity of the organized Europe of tomorrow. The word 'Europe' has become a criterion for membership of the European Union in accordance with article 237 of the Treaty of Rome (1957) and in accordance with the Treaty of Amsterdam (1997). 'Any *European State can become its member*', we read, without the word 'European' being officially defined within it. In the meaning given to it by the Commission, Europe, we have seen, is defined by its content on the basis of geographic, historical and cultural elements which go to contribute towards '*the European identity*', *an identity* which for a large part draws on its legacy of the Age of Enlightenment and on the preponderance of Western civilization. Malta has deferred its decision. The Turkish modernist elite is becoming impatient. Still others, such as the Ukraine are building their strategy of sovereignty on the concept of a 'return to Europe'. Apart from reforms of institutions with a view to managing an eventual assembly of 27 to 30 members States, these aspirants to the Union lead one to pose the question of the limits to be fixed for Europe. There is doubt also over the capacity to build a power able to influence world affairs and capable of peacefully solving crises which remind it of its past replete with conflicts. There is the more commonplace doubt also over the capacity of the Union to revitalize and guarantee the Welfare State.

A more radical doubt is the one that stems out of the deep rumblings of a bad conscience and of guilt, which seem inherent to Europeans. Eugenics in Sweden, ambiguity of the France of the era of Vichy and of the colonies, Christian and Irish violence, the Italian scorn of the North for the South, the silence of the Swiss over a past with its intimations of an ambiguous neutrality—to say nothing of pre-1945 Germany, the Spain of Franco, the Portugal of Salazar—Polish anti-Semitism, as also the implicit demands for amends on the part of the countries of the former bloc now proceeding to return to Europe. A moral doubt was instrumentalized in Prague, by Madeleine Albright, Secretary in the State Department of the United States, who does not wish to see another Munich and thus justifies the selective extension of NATO. The Americans, many of whom fled the European crises, willingly keep alive this image of an Europe obsessed with its past. It is true that from 1850 to 1950, almost 34 million Europeans left the continent, which blunts the postulate of permanent loyalties to the nation. In contemporary times there is doubt in Sarajevo and in Pristina, over the so-called inaction and indifference of Europe to ethnic cleansing. The freedom of others is sacrificed at the altar of the welfare of some. And, it is felt, if it is necessary to act in order to bring order into the world, it is first of all through moral obligation and atonement.

The way things are happening it would seem as if Europe owed a debt to its own history for which it is not truly able to go into mourning and which, perhaps, prevents it from acting in the present. The register of grievances, or rather of confessions and of repentance, is open to the public and everyone in turn can add a complaint, while doubting that it will be heard. However, this game of introspection would not be futile if it were to enable the European debate to be based once again on a study of the differences which seem to block public exchange, whereas they could form its substance if they were to be approached differently.

While the Europe of our dreams is one in which peace and unity prevail, the material realities show somewhat greater contrasts—so great are the conflicts of interests and of actions, in short, differences of visions—the logical results of the basic diversity of the continent at a time when it is attempting an unprecedented convergence of perceptions and projects. Should we deduce from this that the sole response to the European disorder is to be found in the crafting of a new imperial hegemony—which can be the work of a single one alone—by giving in to a new call for an empire, be it a democratic one, or then in accepting to bare the differences, setting them out as realities to be dealt with? The geopolitical bifurcation of 1989 opens a new and still unwritten page in the European process considering that the history of the last half a century is, hereafter, confronted with a wider space necessitating new modes of organization.

CHAPTER 3

Visions of Europe

(GEOGRAPHIES I)

It is the Nation-State which has formed democracy.
Without the reference to national sentiment, there would not be
this marvellous evolution towards democracy and the rule of law.
The nation, a way of going beyond individualism, beyond the corporate
interest, is finally a way of looking at man in civil society.
How to bring the national into European construction,
that is the big question in the European debate.

BRONISLAW GEREMEK (a conversation with the author, Warsaw, 1995)

IS the political Europe, formed after the treaties of the 1950s—an idea older than the project, a spatial mystique, a process of convergence in accordance with the interplays of unity at disparate cadences—old enough, mature enough, to become in turn a historical object, sufficiently well crafted to light up the way to the present and the future?

EUROPE, A NATIONAL PRODUCT

A placing in perspective of this kind stems out of the following interrogation. Is political Europe anything other than the pursuit of their national interests by States which, logically, would emerge strengthened from the community-oriented compromise? Or does it, on the contrary, mark an inescapable erosion of the sovereignty of nations, through successive abdications, for the benefit of a European elite deemed as not being legitimate?

This is the subject of heated debates in France (which is focusing above all on the second hypothesis and ignoring, curiously enough, the first), even though biographies and memoirs exceed in number the works of critical history on European integration. The original, discordant and multi-faceted political conflict between federalists and supporters of the Europe of the fatherlands has undoubtedly contributed towards the lack of historical research in France. The former were insistent on the *doxa*, the Europe of the founding fathers, nurtured on the nostalgia of the idea of a multi-secular Europe. Confronted with the spectacle of the ruins of 1945, they decided to unite their might. The latter preferred to act with discretion so as not to subject their practices to historical criticism. It is from the United Kingdom, the country that has been the most reticent to the European saga, and therefore the one most guarded against hagiography, that the most instructive works have come. These works examine the historical factors of the integration which has fashioned the present day political Europe.

There is a pronounced dissimilarity in the interpretations of researchers, whether historians, economists or political scientists. Some have described the integration as resulting from the growing interdependence of the States signatories to the ECCS, the start of a cumulative institutional logic, with the prospect of a supranational union (Ernest Haas). Others have underlined the resistance of the Nation State and have perceived post-war integration as a means to strengthen it if not to just safeguard it (Alan Milward). Did the starting point emerge only from a convergence of the post-war public opinions facilitating the objectives of integration, the precondition required for a rapid reconstruction and for a consolidation of democratic regimes? Is it to be traced to the memory of the war experience—the humiliating defeat suffered by France, the military supremacy of the German nation—leading the French leaders to contain a divided but democratized Germany within a more durable institution than might be provided by reversible diplomatic alliances? The central role of the Franco-German 'couple' since early times and the notable respect for French initiatives lead to a more strategic reading of recent history. Each partner has derived some benefit from it: 'through the construction of Europe, France aims at achieving a new personality, Germany at redemption'.

The groundwork of a series of acts testifies to this. The Schuman Plan of 1950 (ECCS) aimed at placing the mining and industrial potential of Germany under joint control, so as to arrest any risk of German rearmament, as well as to eliminate any possibility of a permanent occupation of the Ruhr by the Allies. Konrad Adenauer and Guy Mollet arrived at an agreement over the terms of the Treaty of Rome which offered outlets to German industry and to French agriculture. Adenauer sought to strengthen European unity against the Soviet threat (after the Budapest revolt of 1956) and to make sure that the eventual reunification inscribed in the Basic Law would be adhered to by France. In Paris, there was some anxiety over offers by the English of a free trade zone aimed at Bonn (the future AELE), but above all the realization had just sunk in, during the Suez crisis (November 1956) that London was aligning itself with Washington which was refusing to give further support to the French colonial expeditions. A third stage culminated in the Common Agricultural Policy (1962), very favourable to France, and to the signature of the Elysée Treaty in early 1963, two weeks after the French refusal to British membership. A nuclear power, the France of de Gaulle could, by means of this favourable diplomatic bond, keep a watch over the European integration pursued by Walter Hallstein and obstruct in 1966 any decision not taken unanimously (Luxembourg compromise). The initiatives of Helmut Schmidt and Valéry Giscard d'Estaing, in the form of the creation of the European monetary system, imposed on the Brussels Commission, and the formation of a truly executive body, the European Council, consolidated the Franco-German reconciliation. At the same time, the German *Ostpolitik* was making headway (towards East Germany and the satellite countries) and French economy, affected by the two oil crises, needed a greater monetary stability. The later stages illustrate the central role of the Franco-German interaction in European dynamics. The single market and the monetary union were devised, along with a shared will to endorse the anchoring of Germany to Europe, as it would then be obliged to act 'in the name of Europe'. The recent opening up of the German archives concerning reunification (*Dokumente zur Deutschlandpolitik*, 1998) tends to indicate that it was perceived in Bonn that France wanted to obtain the German commitment to the economic union in tandem with the monetary union: it was in Germany's interest 'to put paid to any suspicion of hegemony', while it was in the interest of France to ensure that the link between unification and an enhanced European integration was acknowledged.

While this Franco-German interaction remains the vector of European logics, the community approach is the result of another factor stemming out of the federalist vision of Jean Monnet (in whose biography François Duchêne [1994] reveals also his aspect of an international adventurer comparable to André Malraux). Along with his team, he devised the ECCS, then, based on this innovative model, the EEC. The ECCS was an imaginative response to an American demand that France adopt a coherent policy with regard to Germany. It was essential for Monnet to be on familiar terms with the American elite in order to obtain the support of Washington which wanted to strengthen Western Europe against the Soviet Union. Monnet's objective was to achieve a supranational structure for Europe, to be obtained by 'a continuous process of reforms which can fashion the world of tomorrow more durably than the revolutionary principles so widespread outside the West'. This expert, who was also a pragmatist, was able to give shape to the other, not directly political facet, of the coming together of Paris and Bonn.

On the whole, European integration has been the result of a conjunction of four distinct forces: Monnet's method put at the service a federalist strategy aiming at transcending devastating nationalisms; the American will to strengthen a Western bastion against Moscow; the interest of France in enclosing Germany within a European structure, with the support of other nations (the Benelux countries, Italy) and in regaining its influence in the world; and the interest of Germany in being rehabilitated and in making reunification possible. Finally, it was possible to achieve these distinct objectives because it was in the common interest of all the parties to erect an integrated Europe, a condition necessary for the stability of democratic regimes and for the prosperity of their societies.

The diversity of motivations of the States is a durable reality. It is seen expressed in distinct visions whose idealistic nature is tempered by the confrontation with the visions of the different partners. Each State has its own expectations but there is a striking similarity in their approaches.

In the first phase of European integration, several nations had found themselves confronted with the historical necessity of aspiring to other horizons, vectors of influence other than colonial domination which was coming to an end. This is true for France, which was also seeking in political Europe a substitute for the colonial empire. The Algerian war (1954–62), Suez (1956), the Treaty of Rome (1957), all occurred within this same period. The other sphere of influence was the possession of the nuclear weapon and a seat as a permanent member of the Security Council of the United Nations Organization. But Portugal after decolonization (after the long wars of Angola, Guinea-Bissau and Mozambique) treaded a comparable path. It temporarily abandoned 'the overseas' to turn towards the European continent. Europe is, thus, a club of nations more or less nostalgic over their empires. The exceptions are few (Luxembourg, Ireland). Almost all of them have had to part, more or less long ago, with territorial power (Sweden, Denmark, Austria, France, Italy, United Kingdom, Spain, Belgium, Netherlands, Portugal) or even give up a larger territorial nation (Greece, after the failure of the *Megale Idea*; Germany, with the acceptance of the Oder-Neisse; the Irish Republic after the 1998 agreements, when the claim to a united Ireland was set aside).

Have national interests been sacrificed? Many States of a smaller size and status are finding in the political Europe, based on the principle of equality (and hence with the right of vetoing any decisions considered as affecting vital interests), a guarantee of protection against the hegemonic positions of a particular State or against the widening of the political spectrum granted to an adversary (the case of Greece in the face of Turkey: since its entry in the Union, the economic gap between the two countries has narrowed. The Greek GNP was 50 per cent that of Turkey in 1981 and it went up to 65 per cent in 1997). To prevent the single currency from being closely controlled by the countries of North-West Europe, France supported the entry of Spain, Portugal and, above all, of Italy.

To draw a clear picture of the 'visions of Europe' held by each State is a delicate matter, as it would involve the availability of single criteria and tools of measurement (elites, opinions, parties) which are wanting. It is, nevertheless, possible to sketch the broad outlines of some specific visions.

THE IDEAL EUROPE OF FRANCE

The French concept of Europe is, primarily a political one. The function of the French style Europe, a space for the 'resurrection' of a lost grandeur, is to guarantee and to expand the national power which cannot burgeon alone as was done in the time of Richelieu, Napoleon, Clemenceau or de Gaulle—the haughty guardians of a French centrality paraded with majestic authority. The 'ideal' Europe of France, which delineates the image that other Europeans have of it, manifests itself, first of all, as an enterprise of power. This objective is coupled with the quest for the formation of a multipolar world in which Europe, thanks to its diplomatic initiatives and its currency, would recapture, by the sole magical power of the word, as much influence as de Gaulle would have hoped that it acquire. The dream Europe of Paris remains a 'Europe of realities', that is to say of national States. The European Parliament is less crucial within it, it is believed, than the national Parliaments. It is also a Europe led by the larger countries, even if *ad hoc* coalitions are not neglected. Support is sought from London to maintain the primacy of national States and the specificity of their cultures, to intervene in crises and to conduct a dialogue on nuclear matters. Bonn-Berlin are relied upon to intensify political and economic construction. The worth of the Italian input is beginning to be appreciated for what it is (the Balkans, Western Mediterranean) and also the relationship with Spain (which shares common interests to maintain the modes of community financing). The Europe imagined by France should have a truly economy-oriented government, emerging from the decisions of the European Council and bringing proper balance into the independence of the European Central Bank entrusted with price stability. The single currency will be, from the French point of view, an instrument of power since France will have a say in the matter, whereas till now the currency on which Europe is anchored was logically managed by the *Bundesbank* in accordance with national criteria.

This Europe functions in consonance with an intergovernmental mode, the Commission acting only in accordance with precise mandates fixed by the European Council. It is felt, moreover, that the Commission oversteps its prerogatives. It will never be federal, contrary to what the Germans had hoped till now. It is much more political in its end objectives than the British would ever want. It aspires to wield influence in matters of the world, a far cry from the prudent and moralizing stance of neutrality held by neutral or tiny States. It is interventionist and does not spurn recourse to the use of arms, backed by a solid defence industry, relayed by European alliances. Hence, the idea, accepted by Bonn, of a senior representative in charge of foreign policy and joint security, accountable to the European Council.

In the ideal Europe of France, enlargement is not restricted to Central Europe but also brings in Cyprus, a Mediterranean State, and two countries of the Balkans, Bulgaria and Rumania, just as the recast NATO should include Rumania. Finally, France continues to maintain that a rebalancing of responsibilities be conducted within the Atlantic Alliance, with the objective of parity, by asking that a European be put in charge of NATO's southern command covering the Mediterranean and the Balkans. The ultimate objective is to carve a durable margin of strategic autonomy in the face of the United States but without breaking away from this country: like a 'nonaligned friend and ally', in tune with the lucid phrase used by Hubert Védrine.

Such a vision has to come to terms with that of the other partners. Compromises have been achieved with Germany on several basic points: enhanced co-operation, midway between the 'hard core' with fixed limits, and the rule of unanimity which sometimes blocks avant-garde initiatives. By way of example, there is the European Economic Council in the face of the German demand for a monetary stability pact.

It generalizes a middle position which gives rise to many debates and underlines a contradiction in the French attitude. Do we want a more effective Europe at the price of national sovereignties more inclined towards compromise, or then do we want to maintain a maximum of national influence, at the risk of depriving ourselves of the European lever on the scene of large world-wide negotiations, as also in the management of crises in the areas of interest to political Europe (the Maghreb countries, Sub-Saharan Africa, the Near East)? The first option frightens the French elite for their centralized culture is less open to collective decisions negotiated over lengthy durations of time. The fact remains that till now the European construction has been, in political, economic and financial terms, very favourable to French interests (CAP, regional politics, influence). This contains, moreover, a paradox for France. The political Europe that is coming into being is largely of French inspiration. Yet, public opinion is tardy in acknowledging the benefits that it can derive from it and the advantages that its country has been able to acquire for itself. France remains, nevertheless, perceived by its partners as a 'treasure chest of ideas', an inspirer, with a long line of its functionaries occupying key positions. As Madeleine Albright noted, 'to understand Europe, you have to be a genius or a Frenchman'.

EUROPE SEEN FROM GERMANY

The ideal Europe of Germany, the one it is possible to dream of since unification and the end of the geopolitical tension on its immediate eastern borders, can be stated as follows (Christian Deubner, 1996).

This Europe is first of all an economic union, impelled by a liberal—and social—market economy (with some nuances depending on political sensitivities). This liberalism is regulated through negotiations by the players, while the State does not reject the idea of protecting some sectors of the economy and of society. The single currency will be as stable and as strong as the DeutscheMark and the Council of the European Central Bank situated at Frankfurt (vengeance of the financial metropolis over Bonn, chosen as the capital by Adenauer, a trump card in the face of the City, as well as of Paris and Amsterdam, a balancing act in the face of Berlin, the politico-cultural metropolis) is already attending to this. Ideally, Europe is a federal State, and not a federation of States, with a high degree of decentralization and a negotiated system of financial equalization (in accordance with the modalities of the *Finanzausgleich* which attends to the process of maintaining parity between the *Länder*). The model of the sovereign Nation State is shown as being 'old-fashioned' and the acceptance of this given by the others is a condition for German commitment to co-sovereignty.

Order and liberalism must be extended to Central Europe, and Germany intends to be surrounded by States stabilized by their affiliation to political Europe, as was the case with France after the integration of Spain (only Switzerland remains). The enlargement towards the East, that is to say Central Europe *stricto sensu*, is therefore, an absolute priority. It is, moreover justified by the current interest shown in a 'geopolitical' depiction, of the *Mittelage*, of centrality. Germany, having got rid of the artificial division of the iron curtain, sees itself as situated in the centre of the new Europe. Germany once again finds itself in the middle surrounded by nine neighbours. This gives it the opportunity to take into account the interests of these neighbours when German interests are formulated. The spatial metaphor of the *Mittelage* points to the fact that Germany can no longer be satisfied with the status that it held till 1989-1991 of being the eastern border of political Europe and of Euramerica. Its leaders do not tire of repeating this. In the ideal Europe of Bonn-Berlin, the assertion of centrality consists in instituting, via Europe and on its behalf, a localized order and stability within the first circle of neighbouring countries, in Poland first of all. Internal security—the matter of migrants ('soft security'), and external security ('hard security')—have to be ensured by posting at the frontiers those who will shortly be in charge of border checks (via agreements for readmission of illegal migrants) and through the measured extension of NATO. The proper border is on the Bug, even if it is shown as being transitory. Just as France has been able to ensure for itself, through European construction, a pacified and friendly environment, Germany, for the first time in its history, is now working to achieve this.

In actual fact, this typical ideal is made inaccessible by the ambivalence of certain options. There is a desire to rapidly extend the Union but while keeping its budget at a constant level (1.27 per cnet of the GNP of the fifteen members) and with the exigency of a 30 per cent reduction in Bonn's financial contribution to the Community budget. Then there are the internal debates between Social Democrats and the coalition of the Liberals and Christian Democrats on whether the German model of social market economy is a sustainable one, considering that the large and medium sized firms are massively shifting their locations into Central Europe in order to maintain, through cost reductions, the world-wide competitiveness of the 'German industrial site' (*Standord Deutschland*). There is also the inequality of the economic relations established with the neighbours of the East (a little in the United

States/Mexico manner). A retreat has been noted, moreover, from the exigencies of the European federalist project and the demand has been made for a reform of the decision-making process to bring it more in accordance with the real worth of the States. Acceptance has also been noted of the method of enhanced co-operations, involving less than fifteen States. The differences in orientation of the two large political formations, the SDP and the UCD/UCS have become blurred. Integration within the Union and opening out to the neighbours are the two priorities of both parties; the enhancement of the military responsibilities of political Europe (via the West European Union, WEU) are complementary to NATO. Finally, the integration of the former East Germany, whose society has not known the advantages of forty years of Western and European permeation, presents a wager which will lead to a clearer political commitment from the parties and an increased budgetary stringency (transfers of the extent of 2,000 billion DM since 1990).

The main lacuna in this ideal vision is that it underestimates the role of the national State, which has been given a reduced status in the texts of reference but which remains, nonetheless, a central and legitimate vector of German strategy, notably since reunification. In fact, even if few say it openly, many share the French idea of Europe as a power to be dealt with (declarations of Karl Lamers). The French and the Germans also share the idea that Europe must be organized, unlike the classical British approach.

VARIED VISIONS

In 'Britain in Europe' (Chatham House, 5 April 1955), a speech made before his victory in the elections, Tony Blair had called for an end to Britain's isolation in Europe, through a 'constructive commitment', capable of endowing it once again with influence in the world and breaking away from the image of a 'power that had gone into retirement'. The idea was that it should fully participate in European affairs, in accordance with an old tradition, in such a way as to give them an orientation ('*shaping Europe*'), by building alliances to safeguard Britain's national interests and by combining the sharing of sovereignty with co-operation between governments. The gap between the official reserve and the unsuspected involvement of experts, banks, researchers, industrialists and officials in European affairs is now in the process of being closed. The City will be the main financial market place for Euro deals, while waiting for the Parliament in London to end up by pragmatically adopting this currency.

I could continue to make a tour of the national visions of Europe underlying the commitment of the different States. I will confine myself to some remarks. Thus, in Italy, a founder country, having gained in Europe considerable outlets and a confirmed democratic anchorage, and which has been able to bring reforms into the State in order to become a part of the first circle of the single currency countries, the growing involvement in matters relating to the continent and its approaches needs to be underlined: the Balkans, the Western Mediterranean, the Black Sea region, Central Europe (Poland). European funds should make it possible to consolidate internal cohesion, which depends also on the stability of its environment, for the effects of the crises all around affect first of all the Mezzogiorno. Italy is also anxious that a common order ensures stability simultaneously in Central and Eastern Europe and in the Mediterranean: hence the desire for the military presence of NATO and the policy for a Europeanization of the Mediterranean countries.

I could also make a halt to talk of the Netherlands, another beneficiary of the European Union, a nation of traders which has had the intelligence to make use of its position as an effective interface between Europe and the globalized world and to draw benefit from its proximity to the institutions in Brussels. It is undoubtedly in the peripheral countries that we note the greatest attachment to the cause of Europe. This is so in Portugal, which is equipping itself and coming out of its shell thanks to the funds of the community so that it now maintains relations devoid of any hang-ups with its powerful Spanish neighbour. As regards Austria, its integration into political Europe has conferred on it a larger diplomatic role, and the end of the cold war has served to bestow on it the function of a place of relay for the spaces situated from the Danube to the Ukraine.

Another case is that of Ireland whose integration into Europe has enabled its difficult age-old confrontation with the United Kingdom to be palliated. It can also thus acquire the means for a greater economic autonomy, by serving as a place where foreign investments are welcome. But there is another dimension, which was eloquently expressed by John Hume, a Catholic member of Parliament from Londonderry (Social Democrat Labour Party,

SDLP) and a stubborn mediator, on the occasion of the signing of the Stormont agreements on 22 May 1998, which gave a semi-autonomous status to Ulster. To the question: 'As a European parliamentarian, what place do you give to Europe in the solution of the Irish drama?', he replied:

> After having killed one another for centuries, the Europeans have succeeded in uniting. The French have remained French, the Germans Germans. For me, the European Union is the most tremendous experiment in the world for providing a solution to conflict by the acceptance and the respect of differences guaranteed by institutions and a Parliament. It has broken age-old barriers without victory to one country or another. That's what we are doing here. (*Le Monde*, Saturday, 23 May 1998)

This general survey is a fairly adequate pointer to the fact that national interest remains the primary determinant in the European approach to national States. it should be added that this is also the hope of the political leaders of the 'inner nations'—Scotland, the Spanish Basque country, Catalonia, Galicia, Flanders, etc.—which see in the European ladder a lever to assert their aspirations to a greater sovereignty, leading finally, for the most radical among them, to a formal independence recognized by the Union. What will be, at the start of the twenty-first century, the synchronous conjunction of integrator vectors in political Europe? Over and above the enhanced and widened Franco-German co-operation, depending on the event, and probably supported by the United States (in preference to an American pattern of support focused on Germany alone, which would not have the backing of the other members and candidates), the negotiations for membership will substantiate the soundness of the European approach. The single currency will be a clear token of identity. But nothing indicates that a distinct commitment on the part of civil societies will be achieved, without the establishment of institutional and political reforms (strengthening of the power of a European Parliament finally taken seriously, particularly in France, politicization of the election of the President of the Commission) and unless signs of a European identification are displayed, through the transformation of mediums—education, language, the media—these remain strongly rooted in specific national realities, making them incapable of carrying a European message.

CHAPTER 4

Europe in its Borders, Today

(GEOGRAPHIES II)

Barely do the nations of the West fill
their present contours than Europe looms up
around them and under them, like a backdrop.
ORTEGA Y GASSET (*Ces frontières fatales*, 1930)

THE elimination of internal borders has been among the most common geographic depictions, widely utilized by European elites to illustrate the spatial dimension of the European process.

Although promoted by Jacques Delors, the removal of the barrier of borders was in no way an easy one to the French mind, habituated as it was since time without end to the conspicuousness of the hexagon-shaped patch of France with its sharply delineated contours. The same was valid for England, its insularity confining within it a national culture which for long had preferred to be 'with' Europe rather than within it. The Europe devoid of borders found greater acceptance in Germany. As B. Sauzay has underlined (*Retour à Berlin*, 1998), 'there is not a single intellectual, a single

German politician who does not speak openly of 'overcoming' frontiers (*Grenzen überwinden*), *of transborder cooperation and of Europe of the regions*'. The Germans are more at ease with the fluid logic of networks, whereas the French State gives preference to intergovernmental co-operation, regardless of borders.

It is significant in the mind of the promoters of the idea of Europe that the removal of the barrier of borders, understood here as fiscal and police restrictions, has been considered as a basic 'freedom', one of the four freedoms inscribed in the Single Act of 1986, these being, goods, services, capital and persons. There was a legitimate desire to put an end, in this concerted manner, to the quarrels over demarcations which for too long had pitted the European peoples against each other in age-old civil wars. This is, moreover, why the confines of national States have also become the laboratories for the widening of the political spectrum and nurseries for committed European players.

A single market that has become the domestic market of fifteen members since 1995: the Schengen Space for free movement of people, with ten members, since 1998: the monetary union having a membership of eleven, to begin with, in 1999; common defence projects, associating five or six members. These are some of the areas in which the reality of a Western Europe conceived by its founders as being devoid of internal borders, has received concrete shape: borders to be rendered peaceful through the interplay of economic and political interdependence; borders to be devalued through a strategy of cross-border co-operation and of encouragement to the mobility of men and cultural resources.

THE FOURTH FREEDOM

It was logical that the extension of the areas of market and of flows and the increased exercise of co-sovereignty, in short the sharing of regalian attributes, should involve, *nolens volens*, a profound mutation in some basic border functions. Has there been a kind of political revolution or a simple adaptation that had been rendered necessary by the transfer to the new 'outer' borders of the European Union of functions conducted since long within?

The long duration required for the effective application of the decisions enshrined in the treaties show both the diversity of the criteria and practices of control of the territory and the reticence of the States to part with a basic regalian right. Thus the Schengen Agreement for free movement at the borders of the member States, signed on 14 June 1985, only came into force progressively by 26 March 1995, five years after the signature of the convention for its application.

Paradoxically, it has been much easier to organize the free movement of goods than of persons, as if the latter had become a cause of insecurity in European space. The curbs on the movement of persons was raised to the rung of becoming the main wager in political sovereignty. Such was its extent that it brings to mind the United States with its quotas and its computerized points of entry. The language of the regulation of trade obeys more universal criteria of accounting than that of the definition of national identities. These last are marked by the seal of diversity, which compartmentalization within borders continues durably to express.

The application of this famous fourth freedom brings out an interesting political mutation in this era of networks and free flows. It is less a control over territory which now matters to the political powers than a check over those who claim to move about within it. Should we see in this the crossing over from a territorial sovereignty to a more jurisdictional sovereignty? The technical reply to the question of control over the growing inflows has been supplied by the manufacture of a data processing tool, the Schengen Information System (SIS). This is a centralized body based in Strasbourg for reciprocal, multiple and instantaneous information between the police of the different territories. As for the Keuhl bridge, one can cross it without even a halt since several years.

A DUAL MUTATION AROUND INTERNAL BORDERS

A dual mutation has come about. On the one hand, the border functions have been displaced anew in space. On the other hand, most of the territory is being treated as an expanded border zone. In a multisecular effort, the European State apparatuses had endeavoured to consolidate the envelope of national territories, either by modifying their contours to fix them through wars leading to the mobilization of internal unity, and treaties freezing the new power equations, or by seeking, along a near exclusive line, a spatial convergence of all the functions conducted by political borders. Thus, in the case of France, there were Vauban and Colbert who drew up the basic principles of demarcation of a fortified territory in the face of strategic adversaries and of the strongest among the competitors. At the end of this classic process of political homogenization, nation and territory, currency and market had taken on the same spatial contours. The customs authority, nationalized in 1791, had become the 'immense administration' which, on the eve of the Treaty of Rome, collected 22 per cent of the fiscal revenues of the State and again 17 per cent in 1993 (oil, gas and VAT on extra-community products).

Elsewhere, it was indeed by means of an internal customs union, the *Zollverein*, that the first modern German unification took place, just as it was with the monetary union that the Federal Republic finally evolved in 1949, out of a grouping together of three zones of occupation whose single currency became the Deutschemark. This was extended in 1990 to the former East Germany.

Thus, organized Europe is the regional form of an inevitable process of globalization, the middle courtyard looking after the economic interdependencies that are the guarantor of relationships made peaceful. Economic exchanges in the middle of the present decade exceeded in value 1,500 billion Euros. The customs, a fiscal service and economic agent, no longer has to manage the 'legal routes' through which goods used to cross. The 'customs area' has become greatly enlarged. Also, in order to get adapted to an economy of tight flows and zero stocks, the customs officer operates in every centre of production. There is a spatial dilution of a 'functional' customs, delocalized hereafter over the entire places of actual production for Europe, the domestic market. Credit cards, swift network for circulation of capital, purchase orders by facsimile and telex are bringing fluidity into the financial space. Financial management and control are concentrated in the places from where the orders are placed. The dematerialized economy of services appears to have got the better of constraints of space. On the new French 'customs map', most of the staff is concentrated now at the outer borders of the Union (Switzerland, maritime ports and airports, in this case). The number of customs clearance offices has been reduced in the metropolis. From 375 it had come down to 274 by end 1992. The customs official has become an agent for regulating the national economy (keeping a check on norms, monitoring extra-community trade, confronting infringements). In short, the working space has become interiorized with a view to ensuring economic security.

Other indicators underlining the growing fluidity of the European space are the mobility of degree holders, of students and teachers, to say nothing of the around 330 million tourists who criss-cross Europe, four-fifths of whom are Europeans. Between 1991 and 1994, 11,000 qualified persons holding degrees in higher studies, have been able to work in a country of the Union other than their own, on the basis of a general system of equivalence of diplomas and qualifications. Since 1987, almost 5,00,000 students have moved around in Europe thanks to exchange programmes financed by the Union.

The new complexity in the management of the movement of persons can be assessed with the help of some simple and evocative figures of which most people are unaware. Counting the three modes of access by land, air and sea taken together, the number of persons from the signatory countries of the Schengen Agreement who cross their borders has risen to around 2 billion per year. The traffic from and towards Germany is of the order of 864 million. It is more than 291 million for France. The figures for Spain, the Netherlands and Italy are 120 to 135 million. Of this total the number of persons having crossed through the internal borders of the Schengen space is assessed at 1.3 billion.

Since the signature of the Treaty of Rome, the number of journeys has reportedly multiplied by twenty. In the case of France, three-fourths of the journeys, i.e. those undertaken by around 230 million people, are made by land. To give a detailed breakdown, the air and border surveillance police has kept a watch over fifty posts, as compared to the 762 roads and paths leading to the outer envelope of the border from Dunkirk to Menton and from Perthius to Hendaye. Out of this total number of 'travellers', made up in the large majority, of nationals and of citizens of the countries bordering the Union, only 5 per cent were those who were required to hold visas. A 20 km strip along the French borders has been set up for conducting surprise mobile checks as a necessary counterpart to free movement. The work of checking has become specialized. The surveillance is no longer conducted along a narrow corridor. Surveys have instead been extended to places all along the 'green border' which, in the language of specialized officials, designates the spaces in between the major crossing points. Police forces have been redeployed to concentrate on curbing clandestine networks. Their action is targeted, on a priority basis towards those at the departure point, attempting to cross through, as well as towards those at the destination point, who employ them. Hence, the surveillance system has to be adapted to fit into the spatial logic of networks, while the border aspect at the all the key points of a territory, its core communication points, is diluted.

The application of the Schengen Agreements induces new internal spatial differentiations. Indeed four types of situations are detected. Eight of the ten signatory States have begun to apply the agreements (Germany, France, Benelux, Spain, Portugal and Austria). Two other signatory States, Greece and Italy, have postponed their implementation, the second having begun their application in the spring of 1998. Five States (Ireland, United Kingdom, Denmark, Sweden and Finland) are not signatories.

Hence, within the European Union, a sub-assembly, Schengen, is emerging, characterized by the following system: freedom of circulation for the regular residents of the eight members, whatever be their nationality, including those originating from third countries; uniformization of visas of less than three months (for a list of countries jointly drawn up and in accordance with a single model of visa delivered by the consulates) and joint checks at the outer borders; presence of liaison officers from each country in the neighbouring countries to verify the application of the agreements at the outer borders. Since March 1995, entry into the airports has been reorganized, to separate the flows of traffic according to the place of origin (around 200 million annual journeys).

The United Kingdom has asked that checks be maintained over nationals of third countries. This means that Ireland, which has been free of any checks with its neighbour since the 1920s, will have to await the decision on the British request. Finally, the two Scandinavian States which have an open border with Norway, which is not a member of the European Union, have had to fall in line with the agreements on the passage across this original outer border. The space of circulation has become more heterogeneous depending on the degree of participation in these agreements. As with currency or with institutional reforms, the Europe of the fifteen member countries clearly has a variable geography in accordance with the more or less temporary technical and functional borders. These differences in harmonization also stem widely out of the problematics of the outer borders, in view of the geographic diversification of the pressures of migrations.

BORDER METAPHORS

An attentive scrutiny of recent European history reveals the close correlation between the most spectacular political mutations and the data relating to migrations. Since 1989–90, the migratory space has indeed widened to cover the dimensions of the continent. It is in fact under the effect of a migratory pressure of political and economic significance that the old geopolitical order has collapsed. The breach was opened at the Austro-Hungarian border following the Germano-Hungarian bilateral agreement advantageous to the East Germans, than even to Berlin. The fourth freedom, that of free movement, has been courageously reasserted by East German nationals. Among the first new activities that offices have embarked upon in East Berlin, is the opening of travel agencies, automobile agencies and fashion stores for a clientele thirsting for colourful goods in their eagerness to break away from the dull monotony of the old society. No fashion industry can survive without freedom and the search for individual expression.

The iron curtain had acquired the function of a very effective barrier to migrations towards the middle of the continent, with the exception of the two German States and those States which negotiated and capitalized on the limited departure of their German minorities (Rumania and the USSR). Indeed, one of the objectives of the *Ostopolitik* was right from the start, to help the German minorities to leave (1 million were repatriated between 1950 and 1969, 1.3 between 1970 and 1989), by virtue of article 116 of the Basic Law which defines the wide criteria for reassimilation into one's nationality, on the basis either of a German citizenship prior to 8 May 1945, or of ethnic German affinity.

The raising of a part of the iron curtain decided upon by the Hungarian Government in May 1989, between Sopron and Hegyeshalom, was the result actually of a policy of Germano-Hungarian reconciliation which started right from 1986, when the Government of Janos Kadar 'became aware of the advantages in dealing with its Germans in an exemplary manner' as Timothy Garton Ash (1995) recalls. Hence the grant of an unconditional loan of a billion DM in 1987, 'a sign intended for the other States of the Soviet bloc'. In fact, Bonn was making it known that the new *Ostopolitik* being formulated aimed also at financing the maintenance of its compatriots at their places of residence. But paradoxically enough, the effect it had was to promote both the negotiated dismantlement of the iron curtain and a new migration of its minorities towards Germany with the result that Central and Eastern Europe have never had as few German residents as they have today. This act of repatriation also explains for a large part the fact that Germany received in 1992 two-thirds of all the emigrants leaving for Western Europe. One of the reasons for the German involvement in the external political affairs of the continent is, moreover, a result of this concern (the return of refugees from Bosnia and Kosovo).

MIGRATIONS AND PRODUCTION OF BORDERS

Over and above this specific national situation, the general problematics of migration has reappeared in Europe. While the States of Western Europe have closed their doors since the last twenty years to large migrations of workers, mobility has not ceased for all that, either on account of the specific politico-economic situations prevailing in the countries from where the departures originate, or even on account of the very fact of the restrictive measures adopted in the destination countries, bringing about the grouping together of families and the multiplication of clandestine entries.

Some South European countries from where the departures used to take place have become destinations (Spain for the Moroccans, Italy for the Moroccans and Albanians, Greece for the Albanians). Countries such as Poland are now countries of destination and transit (from West Europe) but also of departure (towards Berlin). The European Union includes around 20 million foreign residents, of which 6 million come from other European States, 4–5 from Turkey and the States that have succeeded Yugoslavia, 3–4 from the Maghreb countries and from Africa, and 1 million from Asia. The change in the migratory data, marked by a constant pressure from the peripheral areas of the Union (Turkey first of all, South Asia, the countries of the Balkans, particularly Albania and Rumania), will lead step by step to the establishment of a policy of quotas, as in Switzerland.

Over and above these findings for which figures are available, one may wonder to what extent the concrete management of the flow of migrants originating from outside the Union does not finally constitute a central element in the definition of the effective borders of organized Europe. Reference can be made here to the German policy on migration. In the framework of this policy, a series of restrictive bilateral agreements have been concluded on the granting of asylum, covering a migratory space whose limits are not situated on the Oder-Neisse but more to the east and the south-east, thus including the States of Central Europe already associated with the Union with the objective of becoming a part of it. Since July 1993, those seeking asylum, coming into Germany via Poland, are sent back to this country which has become a transit point, on condition of financial compensation for the costs involved in the strengthening of border checks and the acceptance of some refugees (Rumanians most of all). Comparable agreements have been signed with the Czech Republic, Hungary and Rumania in 1994, while others are being prepared for signature with Bulgaria (to reduce the numbers arriving from Turkey). The Eastern borders of the States neighbouring Germany, and the States close to the areas of departure are, if the earlier mentioned agreements can be totally implemented, on the way to functioning as migratory limits of the European Union, further extension of its present borders. It is an unstable response to the contradiction between the increased opening up to the interior and the strengthening of the controls on the outer envelope, while at the same time these States are associated with the Union, in a process of transition towards full and total membership.

In the South, the summer of 1998 was marked by a fresh outbreak of attempts, organized by prosperous networks along the Moroccan and Tunisian coastlines, at illegal entry by clandestine immigrants into Spain and Italy, coming from the Maghreb countries. This led the Italian authorities to sign co-operation agreements in August 1998 with Tunisia and Morocco with a view to identifying the migrants and facilitating their repatriation, the costs being borne by Italy. Some financial mechanisms meant for the rehabilitation of the migrants driven back are being examined in Rome. Thus, imperatives are being discovered for a co-development over a border which is beginning more and more to resemble that of the South of the United States.

OUTER BORDERS OF POLITICAL EUROPE: FROM THE DETROIT OF GIBRALTAR TO THE KOLA PENINSULA

From Tangiers to Murmansk, while crossing through Istanbul and Saint Petersburg, we discover the great diversity prevailing in the immediate neighbourhood of the European Union. This diversity is such that the only common element in these greatly dissimilar States, and even regions and cities, is precisely the movement towards the urban and State level poles of the Union, which have become centres of attraction. These neighbourhoods can be classified into seven distinct overall zones, from the south-west to the north-east.

In the south-west, the Maghreb, a kind of western Arab-Berber island between the Mediterranean and the Sahara, has, on an average, a standard of life five to ten times lower than that of the States closest to the Iberian peninsula and to Italy. Their GDP put together represents 4 per cent that of the fifteen. The Union is both their foremost client and their principal supplier, to the point that their factual integration into the community market is more advanced than that of the States of Central or Eastern Europe. The Union is also their foremost financial patron. Contrary to a widespread idea, the 'opening up to the East' has not led to a decrease in the flows of financial assistance coming from Brussels. In fact it is quite the contrary. The direct financial aid granted for 1991–6 tripled as compared to the earlier protocol: 1.425 billion Euros out of the community's budget and 1.4 billion Euros for loans from the EIB (European Investment Bank). This is a deliberate action aiming at giving a new turn to the Mediterranean Policy of the Union, in application of the conclusions of the Abel Matutes report. The November 1995 Conference of Barcelona sanctioned a financial assistance of an amount of 4.7 billion Euros (1995–9). A parallel can be drawn between this figure and the amount of 7.2 billion granted to the Central and East European countries taken together.

At a time when the answer to the questions of how to curb migrations and how to promote growth in the countries which migrants want to leave, appears to lie in the strategy of displacement of the premises of firms. The Maghreb States could be beneficiaries of this policy. But then there comes into play the matter of the competition from East Europe, where the cost of labour is still very low. The Maghreb, a zone where there is a very significant French cultural and economic presence, is also witnessing a more active presence of the Italians and the Spanish, who are making big investments in Morocco since 1991. Thus we see a new strategic association bringing together the nine riverside States of the Western Mediterranean, among these being the five States joined together within the Arab Union of the Maghreb, blocked at present as a result of the Algerian civil war.

There are at least two uncommon factors in this close proximity to the Union. The countries bordering the southern shore of the Mediterranean have no prospect of membership. One might at best talk of a strategy of long term 'partnership', resulting from the setting up, by around the year 2010, of a free trade zone. Moreover, Southern Europe is not the economic partner preferred by the States of the southern shore. They account for only around 28 per cent of their total trade (leaving out power). This is explained by the mediocre transport system in the Mediterranean and the major attraction that north-west Europe presents.

The Maghreb is an integral part of the European geoeconomic unit without being able, as in the past, to export its labour there. The bar to migration is not a small factor in the Algerian social and identity crisis, having ended up today in a civil war, one of whose political wagers is the nature of the relationship with Europe. Two States remain the object of all attention, partly on account of their geostrategic position. There is Morocco, to the south of the Detroit of Gibraltar, and Tunisia, to the south-west of the Detroit of Sicily. The European strategy seems to be ambivalent, but is there truly a desire to see horizontal links developing between the States of the southern shore, perceived as the premises for the formation of an anti-Western political coalition?

Italy, because it faces the Adriatic, has a land border with Slovenia, and complicated relationships with Slovenia and Croatia (the status of the Italian minority in Istria; the issue of compensations to Italians in Slovenia), is directly involved in the Balkanic and Central European problematics. The pressure of Albanian emigrations is a manifest symptom of this. It has been further aggravated by the flood of refugees coming from Kosovo, since July 1998. The Otrante canal, marking the dividing line between the zones where we see one of the greatest differences in standards of life in Europe, magnified by images of the good life, conveyed by Italian commercial television channels, is covered by an Italian aeronaval unit which tracks down the fast launches operated at night by those who make a trade out of illegal immigration. This furnishes a parallel to the American vigil over the coasts of Florida. The Italian State is reflecting over the opportuneness of sending back to Albania the logistic and police brigades entrusted with channelling humanitarian aid and in keeping a watch over the Albanian ports. In Rome itself, it is estimated that the surveillance of the Otrante canal could prefigure one of the missions of the 'Euromarfor', an Italian initiative, bringing together France, Spain and Italy for the joint maintenance of security in the western Mediterranean.

Italy has also had to put up with new States as neighbours, such as the Slovenes who have become independent since 7 October 1991 and for whom some sympathy has been noted in Venezia and in Friuli. The Italian Government had engaged in some active diplomacy in south central Europe, after the initiative taken by the Pentagon since 1989 and extended curiously enough to Poland in 1991 (in a hexagonal formation). This is the framework for a co-operation and promotion of Italian commercial interests to the south of the Danube mainly. Italy figures second among the countries of the Union as regards market share (around 15 per cent) coming just after its main competitor, the FRG.

In the south-east corner of the European continent, the Union is represented by Greece, an isolated State whose immediate neighbourhood is particularly complex and constantly undergoing change. This is so for Albania, Macedonia, Bulgaria, the land and sea borders with Turkey and, over and above these, the issue of Cyprus. In this matter, in principle, the Union availed of a valuable prop. In actual fact, Greek Governments, for reasons of domestic policy, have sometimes appeared to act against their own interests. Otherwise, it would have been possible for Greece to directly extend its influence, at least on the economic plane, to its immediate periphery to achieve its stabilization. Drawing more than 6 per cent of its GNP from inputs from the Community, Greece is undoubtedly a poor relation of the Union but it is perceived by its neighbours as a prosperous and alluring State. There is great pressure of immigration from Albania towards the north-western part of Greece. In Macedonia, the trade blockade which put an end to the Vardar Axis was condemned and people continue to look towards Thessalonica, rather than towards Belgrade. Relations have improved with Bulgaria and there is a constant flow of Greco-Bulgarian trade along the Struma valley. The economy in this region is on the upswing.

Greco-Turkish interaction remains as fraught with danger as ever and the Lausanne System of 1923 is unstable. There is Cyprus, the problem of the maritime and air borders, the future of the 'Muslim' minority of Thrace, the rivalry with Istanbul, the large metropolis of South-East Asia (whose market radius extends today up to Bucharest, Constanta and Odessa, as I have seen from my own on-the-spot observations, and then the Athens/Thessalonica segment). The signing of a customs union between Brussels and Ankara has been finally approved. Greece has obtained in exchange a commitment by the Community that negotiations will be undertaken between the Union and Cyprus in April 1998.

The old logic of power continues to weigh on south-east Europe. The United States desires to extend its zone of military influence (NATO) further towards the north, by including Albania, Macedonia (American soldiers of the United Nations are present with Scandinavians at the Serb-Macedonian border of Kumanovo) and one day undoubtedly, Rumania. This enters into conflict with the dual Russian and Serb preoccupation for maintaining some anti-Turkish alliances in the 'Balkans' (via Bulgaria, that is to say the western shore of the Black Sea) and for setting up a Morava-Vardar (Belgrade/Athens plus Sofia and Bucharest) political axis in opposition to 'horizontal' projects (infrastructures among others), from Tirana to Istanbul via Skopje and Sofia. The end nineteenth century Balkanic 'big game' is still operating, with the result that South-east Europe, in an advanced process of balkanisation, is being constantly left behind in the movement towards integration into Europe. Finally, the Greek Government feels a special sense of responsibility towards the approximately 6,00,000 'Pontus' Greeks, the Greeks of the Euxine (Black Sea), that is to say in the area south of Russia, plans are being devised to receive them at the northern border of Greece.

Hemmed in within the community, Greece, where the Brussels rulings are tardy in application, is, since lately, taking on a new geopolitical importance stemming out of the political changes in Albania and in Bulgaria, the worsening crisis in Kosovo, as well as the development of the crises of partition and of State succession within the Yugoslav space. It is due to this that the Greek Government, the only State of the Union which could be directly affected by a territorial dispute if the Albanese crises were to worsen, would find itself obliged to assert its security interests. Finally, Greece has another geopolitical characteristic which has been inadequately underlined but which could prove to be strategic in a Pan-European policy of the Union. It is indeed the only Orthodox State of the Union, if we consider as relevant the differentiation of the continent into two historical units along religious lines. For the future, the recomposition of Europe involves a dialogue, a difficult one till now, between two very distinct types of societies. Greece may be able to serve in this respect as a 'bridge', a little like the Spain of 1992 was able to make use of its function as an interface between the EEC and Latin America. It is consequently necessary that Brussels strengthen the Greek pillar of the Union in a region having a neighbourhood that is, to say the least, disturbed.

The entry of Austria into the Union, over which it presided for the first time in the second half of 1998, was a logical consequence of the geopolitical bifurcation of 1989. The status of neutrality imposed by the State Treaty of 1955 had turned Austria into a buffer zone between the two blocs. A revision of this strategic middle position began with the 1995 membership. The Austrian borders of the Union touch the south of the Czech Republic, the western part of Slovakia, notably its capital Bratislava (40 km away), as well as the west of Hungary (Budapest is 250 km from the border) and the north of Slovenia. While Vienna is proving to be an excellent urban economic pole, backed by a notable Austrian economic commitment in Central Europe, eastern Austria is prey to the pressures of migration. The result is that the borders are both more open than before and also more guarded. The multinational projects revolving around the Austria-Slovakia-Hungary triple point continue to remain at an incomplete stage as long as the Hungaro-Slovak bilateral disputes are not settled. It is, however, western Hungary (the Gyor region) which is drawing the greatest benefit from the economic breakthrough, along the new Vienna-Budapest highway. This is, therefore, a virtual trans-border space with Vienna, former 'door of the East', enhancing in this area its role of hub and command centre (with 800 head offices of Western and Asian firms; 400 foreign press correspondents covering median Europe). But this enhanced status has to battle once again, as in the past, with the financial ambitions of the Budapest market place.

Austria finally insists on the maintenance of standards by the neighbouring nuclear power stations (Krsko in Slovenia; Bohunice and Mochovce in Slovakia; Temelin in the Czech Republic). The *Ostökofonds*, an Austrian fund for ecology, is working aims towards restricting the pollution emanating from the neighbouring countries.

At the east and south-east of unified Germany, Central Europe *stricto sensu* is made up of four States: Poland, the Czech Republic, Slovakia and Hungary. Seen from Berlin, 80 km away from the Oder-Neisse border, Central Europe is a preferred, but not exclusive, market (an average of 40 per cent of the market share of the OECD countries). It is an area of industrial sub-contracting endowed with skilled labour and it encompasses an assembly of States to be incorporated as soon as possible, but at a negotiated cost to be shared by the other member States. The security horizon is therefore perceived as going right up to the Bug, the eastern border of Poland, the outer limit of political Europe right from the start of the next century, probably for a long time to come.

It has been acknowledged in Bonn since the time of Adenauer, that the recognition of the Oder-Neisse line would be the condition for the support of the Western allies to any reunification of the Germans between the Rhine and the Oder. The waiting period orchestrated by Chancellor Helmut Kohl, to make a public expression in 1991 on this matter was less due to a reticence over the content than to an internal political constraint. 'The strategic design had been to demonstrate to the nationalist right and to the last of the implacable, among those who had been thrown out, that this was simply the price that Germany would have to pay for the unification of the Germans between the Oder and the Rhine. He could then indeed say to the genuinely nationalist revisionists: do you really wish to sabotage German unification?' (Timothy Garton Ash). The ultimate ratification of the final treaty on the borders with Poland in autumn 1991 involved a new Germano-Polish bilateral treaty concerning also the matter of the right of the minorities of Upper Silesia.

The Oder-Neisse border is as unequally balanced, in terms of standard of life, as the one that separates Southern Europe from the Maghreb. None of these States can hope to avail of the considerable financial inputs which are at present enabling the accelerated economic integration of an old neighbour of the Union, the former

GDR. But of all the States of the former Eastern bloc, they are the best 'placed', literally as well as figuratively, to gain from a positive border-effect. Bonn and the *Länder* are strongly supporting the formation of the 'Euroregions' of the upper western Neisse in southern Bohemia (Nisa, Elba/Labe, Egrenis, Sumava). There is great reticence on the part of the Polish and Czech governments with regard to these initiatives which would involve an administrative recasting of centralized countries. However, the financial contributions of the Community (PHARE and the specific CROCO—Cross Border co-operation—programme, for an amount of 150 million Euros per year) for the infrastructures and the improvement of the environment, are to be welcomed. It is neither being contemplated at Prague nor at Warsaw that these virtual trans-border regions would become instruments of integration into the Union nor that they would exclude other forms of local co-operation.

Further to the north, the Baltic Sea, divided even in earlier times by a maritime section of the iron curtain, serves as the framework for a close co-operation between Denmark, Germany, Sweden and Finland on the one hand, and Poland, the Baltic States and north-west Russia on the other hand. The strengthening of the relationship between Helsinki and Tallinn, Stockholm and Riga, has led to the Baltic States becoming the primary beneficiaries of Western support for reorienting their trade towards the West and for a progressive emancipation from Russian domination. There again, the border-effect comes into play, seen particularly in the migration of labourers commuting between Estonia and the south of Finland. The membership of the two Nordic States does not augur well for the formation of a specific community of the riverside States of the Baltic Sea, all the more so as the difficulty that the three Baltic States have in defining common approaches, complicates the coming into being of an organized co-operation. Since the Ronneby Conference, a close association has been forged between Finland, Estonia, the oblast of Saint Petersburg and Karelia, on the matter of environmental protection.

An element to be noted is the fact that the European Union now has a long, direct border with Russia, extending over almost 1,313 km. Finland is interested in the PHARE financing for improvement of facilities for transit (notably towards the Russian Karelia zones of exploitation of forests) and for the environment, particularly as regards the control of the pollution of nuclear origin emanating from the Kola peninsula. To the east of the Vyborg isthmus, the town councillors of Saint Petersburg, as in the past, resolutely play the 'Russian door to Europe' card, competing with Riga and Moscow.

The multiple forms of the border interaction of the Union in its end-of-the-century contours, is applicable to the near totality of the major assemblages of the area of Europe, understood as a geoeconomic space encompassing the western and central Mediterranean, south-east Europe (including Turkey), Central Europe and Russia. These new functional borders are broken up in space. While the realm of geoeconomic relations tends to expand the European space in tune with the extension of market economy, other factors on the contrary are contributing towards restricting it. This has been noted for migrations, Central Europe functioning as a transit point and in fact a kind of filter. The same goes for institutional affiliations, since the high costs of a subsequent enlargement of the Union will contribute to more realistic approaches than those of the public refrain over a future European configuration conceived as being unlimited. Finally, behind the decisions for extending NATO, we catch a glimpse of the silhouette of other boundaries, those of security. What is paradoxical here is the fact that entry into this institution has been proposed for the three States of Central Europe which actually experience the least problems of security.

As formerly, their strategic status is considered in terms of external preoccupations, in this event the security of Germany and the interests of the United States in maintaining their influence in the region. Conversely, Moscow would make do with a *status quo*, the 'security vacuum' felt by some being perceived here as the maintenance of the external sheen of a status comparable to that of Finland or of Austria before 1989. In a continent with its present borders dating to the recent past (half of which date back to the last half a century) and which are sometimes still shifting, if not the object of actual clashes, security can, to begin with, take the form of diplomatic measures for stabilization. This again involves the positive recognition of inherited formations, the drawing up of a multiplicity of agreements for good neighbourliness and concrete local co-operation. A hundred agreements of this type have been signed since 1990 and assigned into the Stability Pact adopted on 20 March 1995 during the Second Conference of Paris. The reference point is undoubtedly provided by the Franco-German interaction. There is, therefore, indeed a modern European model of border interaction whose extension to other bilateral relationships, burdened with a troubled history, is one of the wagers of the setting up of a Europe rid of border lines. The field for negotiated settlements of tragic quarrels over demarcations of borders remains for a long time an open one, in south-east Europe, as at the perimeter of the Russian envelope.

CHAPTER 5

The Variable Geographies of Conceivable Europes

(GEOPOLITICS I)

Enlargement is in the interest of the whole of Europe. We do not wish that it be considered as a work of charity. It is a challenge thrown at Europe. For the first time in its history, it has the possibility of constructing its internal order in accordance with the principles of political and economic cooperation on an equal footing.

VACLAV HAVEL (*Le Monde*, 23 June 1995, conversation before the European Council of Cannes)

FOR forty years, no question ever arose about the borders of European Union Community monopolized the use of the word 'Europe'. Its borders were then distinct, making out the territories of the member countries and those of the few others situated to the west of the iron curtain, the border of alarm.

The other half of the continent was 'East Europe' or even 'the East', an ideological category without any legitimate territorial base. It was only when some dissident and courageous thinkers in Prague, Warsaw or Budapest decided, during the 1980s, to break away from the dominant geopolitics they were subjected to that 'Central Europe' re-emerged as a geographic notion and began to make dents in the iron curtain. As against the strategic and ideological division of the continent, they put forward the argument of the continuity of historical affiliations, the fluidity of cultural expressions, the similarity of architectures. In short, they based their struggle for political emancipation on the will to effect a 'return to Europe', a Europe whose pacts subsequent to World War II had orphaned them. Europe, the real Europe, was likened to a space of freedom.

Since 1989, the democracies of Central Europe have placed new responsibilities on the countries of the Union since, as acknowledged right from the start, any European State could become a member of the Community. But, before being a geographic entity, the Europe we are talking of here is political in nature. How are we to respond to these new demands without jeopardizing the gains of nearly half a century?

DEFINING EUROPE?

When the first requests for membership of the Union were made, the Brussels Commission had to clarify its perspective. The term 'Europe', it said,

> combines geographic, historical and cultural elements which, together, contribute to the European identity. Their shared experience of proximity, ideas, values and historical interaction cannot be condensed into a simple formula and it remains subject to revision by each successive generation. It is therefore neither possible nor appropriate to now establish the borders of the European Union whose contours will get drawn with the passage of time (European Council of Lisbon, 1992).

That is the stage we find ourselves at today. Indeed, since the beginning, European construction has taken place in accordance with a self-maintained evolutive process, without concern for final geographic limits. Today, with the multiplication of the number of candidates (twelve in 1998), the refusal to consider the matter of borders becomes a factor of uncertainty if the final architecture is not sketched. If, indeed, this is humanly possible or even diplomatically desirable. What are the possible answers?

Rather than seek to fix the ultimate lines of demarcation, the Union has defined some criteria for membership. These are: a stable, vibrant and unequivocally democratic regime; the capacity to espouse the Community legislations and adopt the standards laid down by the Union; to withstand the impact of a rapid opening up of their markets to products arriving from more advanced economies and finally, to reform their national administrations. The precondition for democracy has been stated in the Treaty of Amsterdam which asserts that: 'only democratic States, adhering to human rights, fundamental liberties and the rule of law, can belong to the European Union' (Jacques Santer, Strasbourg, 16 July 1997). This battery of criteria was applied at the end of 1997 when five countries were selected for the first negotiations from April 1998. These were three countries of Central Europe *stricto sensu*, Poland, Hungary and the Czech Republic, one Baltic country, Estonia, and one State which had earlier been a part of the former Yugoslavia, Slovenia. Cyprus has been added to the list. A pre-condition is that the negotiations in this regard would include representatives of the northern part of the island. This membership is contemplated as a factor for solving a protracted crisis, with a view to forming a bi-zonal and bi-national entity. The application of political criteria has led to the refusal of membership to Slovakia where democracy is still inadequately applied, particularly as regards respect for the rights of the Hungarian minority. It has also delayed consideration of the request for membership made by Latvia, on account of the conflict between the Latvians and the Russian minority which is struggling hard to obtain citizenship. In the case of Lithuania, it is more the tardy pace of the first reforms that has led to its refusal.

It is difficult to know on what date the first expansion of the Union will take place. It could be between 2002 at the earliest and 2006 at the latest. But already one of the cardinal wagers for negotiation relates to the supervision of the future borders. The Union, on account of its prosperity and the civil liberty that prevails there, has become an alluring centre for migrants. The functions of checks on migrations have been moved to the outer borders, extending from Finland to Spain, of the Union which today has fifteen members. Tomorrow they will be increased to twenty, and the border will extend from Lithuania and Kaliningrad to the boundary between Slovenia and Croatia. Now, the States that are candidates are keen to maintain some right of ingress at their eastern borders, with free local movement, a factor contributing to social modernization and economic activity. This is so between Poland and the Ukraine or Byelorussia. Similarly, the Hungarians refuse to cut themselves off from the co-ethnic communities of Slovakia, the Ukraine and Rumania. Conversely, some countries such as Austria, Germany, Finland and now Italy, are asking for the application of greater restrictions on migrations. A divergence is noted here between the policy of the Union and the national interests of the candidate countries. The Union wants its future outer border (that of the first expansion) to be first of all secure and relatively closed. On the other hand, Poland and Hungary want to maintain solid human bonds at their eastern borders.

Be that as it may, a first fairly effective criterion for fixing the borders of the enlarged Union is becoming more apparent. This will be based on security needs and restrictions on migrations. The nearest candidate States, but which have not been included in the first phase of enlargement, are criticizing the risk of the formation of a new cleavage, of a *limes*, a word borrowed from the border security policy of the Roman Empire.

This differentiation has become strengthened with the American decision to widen the Atlantic Alliance, better known by its acronym of NATO, to the already mentioned three countries of Central Europe: Poland, the Czech Republic and Hungary. The candidature of three other States, Slovenia, Rumania and Bulgaria has been rejected. In 1999, the security border of Western and Central Europe will be established on the river Bug and at the limit between Hungary, Rumania and Bulgaria. By emphasizing their radical opposition to the inclusion of the three Baltic countries in the Euro-American security system, the Russian elites have, in a way, etched a border zone between Russia and NATO, from the shores of the Baltic Sea to those of the Black Sea, since the same refusal is valid also, as seen from Moscow, for the Ukraine and Moldavia. These States in turn are denouncing the risk of the maintenance of a 'grey zone', an unsatisfactory in-between area, presuming that Russia's present weakness is a temporary one.

South-east Europe, which corresponds to the Balkan region and Turkey, remains a zone where indecision prevails. The persistence of national conflicts, manifested by border demarcation disputes that have not yet been resolved, in the area extending from Bosnia to Kosovo, the dilapidated state of their economies and the slow pace of reforms, have contributed towards marginalizing these territories. Yet, these are the areas which, more than any others, needed solid European perspectives, considering that durable democratic regimes could function there. We find ourselves here in a sphere on the periphery of the European Union.

THE EUROPEAN CARTOGRAPHIC ILLUSION

Around 1957, Jean Monnet had been in a position to declare that the borders of the first Community of six members had been fixed not by the Member-States, but by those which had declined membership. It is the antithesis of this situation that prevails now. Joining the Union appears to be a desirable objective and a political priority for a growing number of countries of Central and Eastern Europe. This impetus is deserving of the road that has been traversed, designated under the French concept of 'Community gain'. The Union functions as the 'vanishing point', the perspective of a pictorial scene in which everyone wants to figure, in order to contribute towards carving out an order which in this case is less aesthetic than geopolitical, and where peace has been restored.

While the European perspective gives a meaning to the substantial efforts deployed by the newly democratic countries which want, and this may not happen again, to freely choose their alliances, it is important to clear a cartographic illusion, at the risk of seeming reticent in the face of this revolution. It is hardly realistic to think, in the next decades, that the Union, whose construction has involved forty years of political investment, aims at covering, *in fine*, the entire continent, assuming even that some final borders can be assigned to it. Such an evolution would clearly mark the end of Europe as a process of political convergence that has been mastered. It would establish a parallel between the Union and an ineffective version of the Council of Europe, an admirable institution which functions as a filter of democracy, but whose means of action have become limited. To adopt such a point of view goes counter to many imprudent declarations. I do not wish to suggest that Europe should be recast and that the European Union is finally synonymous with the 'continent'. The conceptual solidity of the notion of continent, which connotes continuum, is moreover doubtful, when one examines actually observed historical solidarities. Its geographic depiction, of a land space surrounded by seas, has little meaning when viewed by history and geopolitics. The historical vitality of transatlantic links like the importance of Euro-Mediterranean interactions, yesterday as today, are proof enough of this. Such a process, promoted undoubtedly by the use, primarily, of maps, proceeds from the superstition of the geographer forgetful of historical and geopolitical processes. Such an objective would lead inevitably to a regression towards the Europes of the past, with their interplay of alliances and counter alliances. We know what disasters they have led to! It is, moreover, significant that in the line of argument evolved by the authors of the CDU-CSU on the future of the Union (*Réflexions sur la politique européenne, CDU/CSU-Fraktion des Deutschen Bundestages*, August 1994, Karl Lamers and Wolfgang Schaüble), the risk has rightly been pointed out: of Germany drifting towards a dominant position in North-west, North and West Europe, and of France in south-west and South Europe. Hence, the proposal for a 'hard core', a 'Kern Europe', with a Franco-German base.

Let us, therefore, stop referring to the European Union only in terms of enlargement, as if it was a matter of an ancient and disastrous political geography (the Congress system? Versailles? Potsdam?). Since the last forty years, a new geopolitical organization has been raised, having enabled an assemblage of sovereign States to get together and jointly exercise their powers on the basis of common, approved, legitimate and evolutive institutions. We cannot accept that political Europe become hackneyed, through dilution, to become a multilateral organization like any other, empty of substance and acquiescing to a law of decreasing yields, a negation of the effort at integration.

The future enlargement of the Union cannot imply that the progress accomplished will be called into question. It will involve a slow process during which the candidate countries will adopt the gains themselves which will continue to be enriched (its existing manifestations being the crossing over to a single currency or the development of a joint defence system or of foreign relations: development aid, humanitarian action). The negotiations launched on 31 March 1998 with six of the candidate countries do not relate to the gains of the Union but to the modalities for membership. Considering that the Union functions as a 'pole of stability', its enlargement can be undertaken only on its own conditions, laid out in keeping with the already mentioned criteria (those of the

European Council of Copenhagen of June 1993). Contrary, however, to the very selective extension of NATO, covering just three States, the Union has committed itself to the entry of all the States that have already presented their candidature, on the basis of some fixed criteria: 'All [the candidates], in the order in which they have presented their candidature to the Union, Hungary, Poland, Estonia, the Czech Republic and Slovenia, in addition to Cyprus [the other candidates are: Lithuania, Latvia, Slovakia, Bulgaria, Rumania and Turkey] are foreordained to become full fledged members of the European Union' (Jacques Santer, Strasbourg, 16 July 1997). The process of enlargement has been understood as being an 'inclusive approach'.

THE POLITICAL END OBJECTIVE

This 'political end objective' aims at enhancing the gain of integration and, in tandem, at enlarging its geographic field to the countries and societies which desire it and are in a position to fulfil it. This vast, in some respects 'engineering', operation, reminds us of past periods of European history, when technical, cultural, political and philosophical innovations were spreading out from the centres of creation. If we pursue the comparison, would it not be a new form of '*translation*', emanating from Western Europe in the direction of those parts of Europe which, after their claim to hegemony, leading to fascist interludes and wars, had been cut off from the most beneficial developments?

In these regions of the continent, notably Balkan Europe, which had neither known the Renaissance, nor the Age of Enlightenment nor, before the communist era, the Industrial Revolution, the road to be covered is long. Similarly, the slow processes of national formation may follow the same route of 'translation', from the former nation States of the western part of the continent towards those which either renew their ties with a lost sovereignty, the Baltic nations, for instance, or rediscover a rejected identity, the typical case being that of the Ukraine and, in a way of Russia, or these that are still at the zero degree of national conscience. An example of the last is Byelorussia, subjected to the vagaries of a ludicrous President. Finally, in some cases, the contradiction between the fixing of national borders and the redefinition of identity obstructs any real democratization. This is so in Serbia, thus, keeping this geographically European country out of political Europe. This translation, in its harshness comes in addition to the already accepted efforts at conducting what has been called the 'transition', a concept borrowed from the Spanish experience after 1975. For Central and Eastern Europe, this process is like that of a modern Renaissance.

This 'translation' does not mean that the candidate countries have nothing to contribute to the Union such as it is. In addition to the fact that the requests for membership oblige it to carry out in-depth reforms, in the modes of decision, in making the procedures and deliberations more democratic, in the allocation of Community funds, several candidate countries also, on account of their position and their national interests, will in turn contribute to security and serve as relay points for the already mentioned transfers of modernity. Poland has evolved a veritable eastern policy with regard to its neighbouring countries, Lithuania, Byelorussia and above all the Ukraine and, beyond it Russia, its neighbour through Kaliningrad. For the Poles who have remained sensitive to their old borders, the lost eastern territories extolled by C. Milosz, the wager lies in responding to the geopolitical uncertainties linked to the (temporary?) weakening of Russia and to the hazards of the political and economic transition in the Ukraine. A way has to be found, of reconciling the impending entry into the Union and into NATO and the development of bonds with these countries in search of sovereignty, in such a way as to consolidate it. Poland is, from this point of view, one of the rare candidate States which are in a position to straightaway participate in the formulation of a geopolitical vision of the Union *vis-à-vis* Eastern Europe, that is to say the first circle of non-member countries. Its participation in the Weimar triangle, with Germany and France, takes on an additional significance in this context.

ELEMENTS OF A PROSPECTIVE: THE INTERPLAY OF SCALES AND DOVETAILED UNITS

At this point of argument, it becomes opportune to sketch for coming times, a hinge and joint model, coupling political Europe, the Union, to 'geographic' Europe which, according to the classic method of the interplay of scales, separates a partially dovetailed unit from its assemblies and sub-assemblies.

The task is an arduous one. Any prospective worth the name should be able to determine some stages in time, some horizons—2002? 2006? further beyond?—and to keep in mind the hazards and risks of regression. The sudden appearance of an unforeseen event can upset the most lucid plans, as Hannah Arendt reminds us. It is not a matter of geography, as if, in an almost geological manner, the territorial expanse determines the end. But the geographic method will help throw light on the wagers and clarify the proposed plans of action.

It is important to consolidate what has been constructed since almost half a century. This is not only of current interest to its participants, but serves as a reference and a point of anchorage for the others. It is proper, moreover, to include in the definition of political end objective another scale, a planetary one, since the Union is not a variable, independent of the mutations taking place in the vast world (subject of Chapter 6).

As for the outer limits of political Europe, it seems demagogic to elude the question or to have it believed that each State will join the Union as if it was a matter of just another ordinary multilateral organization. Its efficacy would then tend to decline. It would also be a factor of destabilization to denote conclusively that Europe must be organized in keeping with a binary logic of inclusion/exclusion.

In the model, in its systemic meaning, that has been sketched out, the present Union is considered as a pedestal, a central referent. Not primarily because it is necessary to view the geopolitical organization of geographic Europe solely by the yardstick of the interests of the founder countries, even though this perspective should not be neglected, either at Paris, Bonn-Berlin, Rome or London. It is also because, globally, the outcome is a positive one. The Union has been capable of inventing a model of co-operation between Nation-States that is unique in the world and that works (see Chapter 6). This limited experiment hence deserves to be spatially expanded. Many of the elite of the candidate countries are, moreover, impelled by the desire to participate in it. But nowhere is it written that inclusion in the political Union is a right.

A model is constructed, therefore, in accordance with a geographic method which does not consider Europe the object, as a whole, with no regard for its objective plurality, but as a set of distinct assemblies and sub-assemblies of different scales: a multiscalar model, or to put it less technically, a dovetailed one, in the likeness of nests of dolls. Four spatial levels have been identified as props for practical action.

Level I: Political Europe: The Scales of the Union

Let us examine first of all the inner dimension. As political Europe becomes larger, it becomes more heterogeneous. Already the jump from twelve to fifteen has eliminated all conviviality within the European Councils. A commonality of interests seems less visible. Over and above the reforms in institutions, modes of decision (qualified majority rather than unanimity) and financing, we see the ushering in of the practice of 'enhanced co-operations' (in accordance with mechanisms defined in the Treaty of Amsterdam). This method enables member States which so desire to go ahead and conduct joint actions without hindrance from the others, but without causing cracks in solidarity.

In short, the States of the Union are not all committed at the same time to the same decisions. This has resulted in some limited unions. The geography of the Euro is different from the geography of the Schengen. The countries that are a party to the single currency have applied the formula of reduced integration to the countries that have volunteered to accept it. These are only eleven out of the fifteen States. The same applies to the field of the industries related to defence, concerning a maximum of five to six States (France, Germany, Italy, United Kingdom, Sweden, Spain). Those European States competent in the matter of security and capable of involving themselves in the management of crises on their 'doorsteps' are fewer than those participating, for instance, in the common agricultural policy. This diversity of commitments should neither shock nor startle. Even London, the City, in spite of its refusal to adopt the Euro, will be one of the central marketplaces for transactions between the Euro and other major foreign currencies, while several countries of Central Europe will cross over from the Dollar to the Euro as the main currency for their trade. Central and Eastern Europe will conduct a smaller number of their dealings in Dollars and will participate in the new 'Euroland'.

And this basic fact needs to be accepted, this fact of a geography that is variable, both on the historical as well as on the political plane, that is to say a geography in the making, even if uncertainty sometimes deprives us of a degree of intellectual comfort. The sub-assembly of enhanced co-operations functions in fact as a vanguard and it is necessary that for the cohesion of political Europe, France and Germany at least should participate in the near totality of its initiatives. Although this sub-assembly is the smallest in terms of number of States, it remains the driving force for European construction. These States, thus, sketch out the European Republic: a space for joint political and economic management.

Numerous affiliations and a too great and ill-controlled extension of the Community of the Union would hurt the cohesion of the European System in which the founder States have put so much effort since almost half a century. The principle of enhanced co-operations aims at ensuring that a sort of core or driving force subsists within the European system, bringing together France and Germany to begin with, so as to avoid the reconstitution of the large or small 'pacts' of the past.

Level II: The Scales of the Enlargement: From Application to Full Membership

In the view of many applicant States, the ideal Union would encompass fifteen plus twelve members, that is to say twenty-seven, within short intervals. To these would be added the States which have not yet crossed the step of explicit candidature. The real Union will undoubtedly be different, in its initial phases.

It will be recalled that since June 1993, certain criteria for membership have been fixed. In December 1994, at Essen, some strategies prior to membership were defined. In June 1995, the European Council of Cannes fixed the outer framework of the PHARE Programme. In December 1995 the Madrid Programme committed itself to starting negotiations six months after the end of the intergovernmental Conference on the reform of institutions which closed at Amsterdam. The European Council of Luxembourg adopted Agenda 2000 (strengthening the policies of the Union, adopting the best approach towards enlargement, setting up a financial framework).

A first sub-assembly was formed by the five countries which, being involved in the membership process, undertook negotiations, while subjecting themselves to a screening of their situation on the basis of the Community legislation. The case of Cyprus is somewhat special, on account of the diriment impediment of the partition of the island since 1974. It is hardly clear what interest it would serve the Union to accept half an island and to have a front line as an outer border.

Their membership will probably materialize before 2006, marking the end of a fiscal year. A period closer in time is possible in the event that the Union will have approved its internal reforms for greater effectiveness, and that long periods of special dispensations will have been negotiated (agriculture, regional policies, environment, free movement of persons). It may be recalled here that memberships made in haste (Greece) were badly negotiated and that the memberships prepared more carefully (Spain, Portugal) over longer periods of time, have passed through crises that have proved to be beneficial.

One question then arises: will the time period between the first and the second enlargement be short or, on the contrary, prolonged? In the second hypothesis, which could be justified either by a reticence of public opinion in the Union (migrations of low cost labour; persistence of unemployment; tendency to withdraw into oneself; international financial crises; budget constraints), or by delays within the concerned countries (where conciliation between efforts of transition and those of preparation for membership would be too burdensome), the outer border of the twenty-nation Union of 2002–6, would risk getting durably consolidated. This scenario should not be dismissed, all the more so, as the new outer border would conform to the peripheral zone of historical Central Europe, nurturing many limiting arguments. Moreover, it is probable that these countries would be in a position to adopt the Euro at the end of this period. This is already the avowed objective of the Polish Government (which has fixed for itself the time limit of 2006). Three of these countries will be participating in NATO from 1999, on account of the effectiveness of their lobbies in the United States, if for no other reason. This will enhance the propensity of foreign investors to come and establish a hold there. Finally, several among them will be active in common external policies, including those concerning the defence industry (Poland, Hungary). In short, the inclusion of this sub-assembly risks bringing about an increase in the distance from the second one.

This second sub-assembly is the one involving the majority of the other candidate countries, which have to face obvious economic, political and institutional wagers. This is all the more so as they have embarked more tardily on the transition as a result of internal political resistance.

These two sub-groups would increase the area of the Union by one-third, its population by 29 per cent and its gross product by 8 per cent only. This latter figure brings out the present disparities. The countries which have pushed their reforms furthest have reached incomes equivalent to between a quarter and half of the Community income (31 per cent exactly in 1997, an average which masks disparities ranging from 37 per cent for Central Europe to less than 20 per cent for the Baltic countries and the Balkans. According to the current rate of exchange, indicative of the salary levels, the figure is only 13 per cent). But it is estimated that around 2010, the five Central European countries will have an average income comparable to that of South Europe, calculated in parity of purchasing power.

These two sub-assemblies and the Union of 1998 are, nevertheless called upon to form a virtual unit, not of institutions but of political consultations. This unit was inaugurated in April 1998 in the form of the permanent European Conference, which met in London (despite Turkey's defection). It is a multilateral consultative framework which has designated its own agenda of discussions (migrations, internal security, transport, etc.). This conference is invested with crucial importance for the future as it fills a gap which is both spatial and temporal between the pole of stability of the Union and the ideally enlarged Union.

Level III: The Sphere of Direct Interest of Europe: The Scales of Geoeconomic Interaction

While security and checking of migrations, the degree of anchorage to democracy and the level of economic modernization are clearly the objective criteria for fixing the borders of the Union for the coming years, other relational factors are seen on the scale of the continent. Thus, a space for very extensive trade exchanges has come into being, since the Union has become the foremost economic partner of the near totality of the States of the continent and also of the countries of the east and the south of the Mediterranean, often with more than half the total trade of each country.

Russia also partakes of an European geoeconomic area, with trade that has tripled since the last five years to reach 45 billion ECU. Economic Europe—for instance, there is the economics of energy which includes Russia (Greater North and Central Siberia) and, in a short while from now will encompass the countries of the Caspian Sea—has, therefore, an area larger than that of the single market. The majority of the countries of the southern and eastern shores of the Mediterranean Sea also partake of this zone of geoeconomic influence. The Union is their foremost trading partner and generally the foremost donor of aid (notably in favour of the Palestinian Authority).

In matters of energy, this is a logical scale. The Union depends for 50 per cent of its energy on external sources and this dependence will increase to 70 per cent to 90 per cent around the year 2020 as regards oil, natural gas and coal. It is partly with Russia, Kazakhstan and the Caspian Sea countries as also with the Middle East that a guaranteed supply has to be negotiated (a treaty was signed in April 1998 for the European Charter for Energy). The same applies to the development of transport corridors and to the TRACECA programme, extending from Caucasia and Central Asia going towards western Europe. It is financed by TACIS (the Baku meeting of August 1998), which is entrusted with the partnership and co-operation agreements signed between the Union and the ten countries of the CIS (Confederation of Independent States) and which also finances the Democracy Programme (promotion of pluralism).

From this point of view, the area under consideration extends far towards the east. A Europe then from the Atlantic to the Pacific? This would mean ignoring the fact that the Russian far east already has one foot in the Asia-Pacific sphere (Korean, Japanese and North American investments, and Chinese workers and traders). Moreover, the Chinese influence is growing on its northern and western borders, notably in Kazakhstan. The areas possessing energy reserves and situated to the east of the Ural mountains are, thus, found located within zones of economic influence having the opposite orientation. It is therefore not possible to indicate where the zone of separation between the two extreme poles will be situated.

This space of interdependence includes the Mediterranean countries participating in the conferences of Barcelona (1995) and

Malta (1997), where the matter of the creation of a free trade zone by the year 2020 was brought up. The MEDA programme has provided for a financial aid of 4.7 billion Euros from 1995 to 1999, as compared to the 7.2 for Central Europe.

This level III corresponds to a sphere in which the Union is interested, within the larger geographic Europe and the Euro-Mediterranean whose stability is crucial to it. Proof of this lies in the fact that it corresponds to the area covered by the PHARE, TACIS and MEDA Programmes. These clearly outline the region to which the Union gives priority with relation to its geopolitical interests.

Level IV: Geographic Europe and its Approaches: A Strategy of Rapprochement and of Pan-European Agreements

Between levels II and III, one scale is lacking, the one which would make it possible to establish a strategy of rapprochement ending in a relationship of real partnership between the Union and some States having an obvious strategic importance. These States are Russia, the Ukraine and Turkey (in the event that the Union would persist in seeking a formula other than full membership for a country often perceived in Brussels as 'Eurasian'). Even though these countries in transition have been marginalized in economic terms—the GNP of Russia, a poor power, is barely higher than that of Switzerland, and that of the Ukraine than that of Portugal—their importance in terms of population, history and geopolitics leads to the belief that the interaction would be a positive one.

After 1991, one could think in terms of a bipolar structure, the two poles being the Union and the CIS. But the symmetry is only an apparent one, keeping in mind the differences in their economies—that of the Union is fifteen times larger than that of the CIS—as also the state of the political systems. There is also the factor of the uncertainties which bedevil this mass of population which has been inadequately polarized by Russia.

The arguments in favour of a more ambitious vision of political Europe, which would end up by encompassing Russia, are not wanting. It is in Europe's interest to show the way towards the transition to democracy in Russia in order to prevent the present social and institutional crisis from playing into the hands of nationalist forces, such as those that took place in the Germany of Weimar. Then there is the reminder of its historic role as a buffer zone between Europe and Asia. Russian demographers describe these as zones of high demographic pressure (Anatoli Vichnevski), presenting a threat to a zone of low pressure, Russia. It could find a place within the European mechanism for checking migrations, in the face of the Islamo-Chinese worlds. There is the factor also of the Europeanity of Russian culture, of its economic history (participation in the Hanseatic networks; opening up of the Baltic by Peter the Great) and of its religion (which is true also of the two Christian States of the Caucasus). This is an opportunity to convert Europe into a demographic power (with a population of 700 million) and a territorial power (including Russia's reserves of raw material) worthy of a continent.

Apart from the fact that no request has been presented (why then give an answer today?), the main objection to Russia's inclusion in the political Union arises from the fact that the Union would find itself highly asymmetrical and that the insertion of Russia would not straightaway add to the power equation. It would be necessary, first of all, that Russia regain its prosperity and carry out its reforms successfully, that it define with greater firmness its national identity, that it complete its self-decolonization and determine its southern borders. These last three elements do not come within the competence of any action to be taken by Europe, which can only facilitate the task by showing that it has done away with any strategy of isolation and contention, that it has removed the sanitary cordon in median Europe and that it guarantees the security of the western portion of Russia. As long as these conditions are not achieved, Europe would come out weakened. In the immediate future, it is admissible to bind Russia more closely to political Europe through a grid of treaties and agreements on disarmament and co-operation, which can evolve into regular practices of political consultation (France/Germany/Russia; Russia/EU) and into political interventions (of the contact group type which join together the United States, Russia, France, Germany, Italy and the United Kingdom, over matters concerning Bosnia and Kosovo), in liaison with the United Nations.

However, at a more distant future, the relations between Russia and political Europe would be dependent on the situation concerning Russian interests, both on its southern flank (Caucasia, Central Asia) and on the Chinese border. It is not unlikely, that Russia, finding itself facing a threat in these peripheral areas (75 per cent of Russian territory with less than 30 million inhabitants is situated to the east of the Urals), might then desire to come closer to the EurAtlantic security structures (including by way of participation in a renovated NATO, extending from Vancouver to Vladivostok).

The Ukraine, surprisingly enough, is another important State in the process of consolidating its sovereignty without major tensions *vis-à-vis* the present Russian leadership. It is not rare to flaunt in Kiev, under the influence of Polish strategists and the postulates of Bzrezinski (*Le Grand Echiquier*, 1997), a desire to assert a Central European identity, distinct from the personality of the 'big eastern neighbour', Russia. Apart from the fact that this depiction is historically correct only for Lviv in the western Ukraine, and that it is more risky to apply it to the main cities of the country, the magnitude of the economic and social links with Russia also should not be ignored. They cannot but put a check on the will to marginalize Russia, which activates the American strategists, who support the Ukraine (third among the beneficiaries of aid coming after Israel and Egypt). To make the Ukraine the central element of a strategy of dissension against Russia corresponds perhaps to the views of American defence and oil circles interested in gaining access to the resources of the riverside States of the Caspian Sea, but does this really further the interests of political Europe? What good would it serve that costly funds be invested in the Ukraine and in Russia—TACIS, BERD—and that at the same time differences become more pronounced between Moscow and Kiev? One of the factors which counters the validity of this approach is the observation of a familiarity, if not a connivance, between the leaderships of these two countries. They share not only the same language of communication and are commercially intermeshed, but they even desire a national redefinition, an upward way out of the Soviet heritage.

Although Turkey is a candidate for membership of political Europe since 1963, bound to the single market through the customs union of 1995, placed by its migrants within the West European labour market and led by modernist elites which have in fact chosen to lean towards Brussels, and Washington, it also falls within this phase where thought has to be given to the suitability of its place in a stable and viable Pan-European space. This is not to disavow its pro-European action but to bring out its objective geopolitical situation which has a parallel with that of the earlier two countries. The arguments in favour of an integration of Turkey into political Europe are many in number. To consider only two among the best known, the geographer will assert that it would be absurd to leave out of the European system Istanbul, one of the big metropolises of the continent, whose range of influence, as an emporium, extends into south-east Europe and up to the Ukraine, in Azerbaijan and Central Asia. It will be pointed out also that if organized Europe is something other than a 'Christian Club', the Turkish input will add to the objective cultural dimension which, in any case already exists in the Union. However, a pessimistic scenario—a take-over of power by a durable Islamist coalition—brings to mind a kind of new 'take-over of Constantinople', as in 1453. The maintenance of a European perspective serves obviously to strengthen the weight of the modernist elites, at least partially. They should be more appreciative of the fact that political Europe is not a simple multilateral organization, with limited functions, but that it corresponds to a zone of historical convergence of societies and of political practices.

Even if these States, essential from the point of view of history, population and strategy, have also become 'peripheries' of the European pole, as is indicated in their comparatively limited economic worth (the total economic worth of these three States, Russia, the Ukraine and Turkey, is less than that of the Benelux) and their low level of development, their geopolitical situation calls for a strategy aimed at giving a greater thrust to the development of their economy.

Several models have been suggested. One of these lays emphasis on matters of security and suggests a Pan-European security organization or a Council for European security, more effective than the OSCE and freed from North America's imperious domination (J.F. Drevet, 1997). Another model is more institutional in nature. Indeed, over and above a Union that has implemented reforms but whose size is regulated, a larger family could be constituted of European peoples sharing a common destiny, its institutional form being that of a flexible 'European confederation', a democratic version of the 'town hall'. This postulate was developed in a recent report of the Parliamentary Assembly of the European Council (1998), which recaptures the geopolitical forethought of François Mitterand, set out already in December 1989 and developed in Prague in 1991. It was perhaps premature at that time as the Soviet Union was not yet dead. It committed, in the view of some, the mistake of keeping the United States out and of being understood as a waiting room by the countries of Central Europe. The approach sketched out was undoubtedly too legalistic or institutional in nature. It is, however, to date the only institution that has been formulated which takes into account a geopolitical vision of the continent as a whole, without making a clean sweep of the valuable gains made by political Europe, and which gives an answer to the lacuna observed between the final enlarged Union and a Europe reduced to its simple geographic or geoeconomic expression. This perspective was formulated anew by Klaus Hänsch, former President of the European Parliament, in March 1998, during a speech before the French Senate. He brought up the scenario of a 'charter of confederal collaboration' with the larger countries at the periphery of political Europe.

Various configurations can be thought up and given varied names, on condition of their starting point being the concrete needs of political dialogue (security, management of changes and crises), of economic interdependence (networks, energy) and of cultural exchanges (training) which weave together the interactions already at work in geographic Europe. A more systematic formula of regular meetings between the countries of the Union already gathered together within 'enhanced cooperations', and the leaders of Russia and the Ukraine, would be desirable. The same is valid for Turkey. It would even be one of the points of application for the joint external policy. Each one would find its place in this 'Europe of spaces', corresponding to the geographic Europe, including hence the margins, which are also the 'steps and markets' of the European Union, including the Ukraine, Turkey and Russia, without affecting the solidity of the integrated driving force of the Union. This pragmatic approach is a way of rationally organizing the European space, without striking a blow at the solidity and the equilibrium of the Union conceived in 1957 and which must assert its nature as political Europe.

THE BORDER ZONES OF POLITICAL EUROPE: A NEW PROBLEMATIC

In these scenarios—sphere of partnership, system of security, a more formalized unit—the problematics of the borders of Europe changes its nature. The borders of Europe in the making are not clear limits, but a 'zone', an area of transition, a thinning out. This gradualism would, moreover, be in keeping with the long duration of European history, with relation to the periods of *translatio*.

Clearly, the limits to be taken note of when formulating the organization of the European space—changes, networks, energy, security—a distinctly geographic matter, are different from those grouping together the driving force of the European project since the start, the geopolitical question. Europe is not defined as a geography pre-existent to any collective action, confined within comfortably distinct limits, but as a historic process inscribed within a space having a variable geography: the meeting of a space and a project, Europe. The project Europe, in the meaning of the democratic process of political and social convergence, is composed of those who wish to and can fully participate in it, if it serves their joint interests, by strengthening the Union.

These four levels, therefore, have their own logic. They only dovetail into each other partially. This dovetailing joins together various 'strata', at different speeds of evolution and in different geographic fields. The observation of the different strata, synchronous but partially overlapping, which form the structure of contemporary Europe, shows us that their limits do not coincide. Variable geography is the only pragmatic path for the management of different spaces, made of centres, steps and peripheries, marked by the seal of uncertainties.

It is fitting to add, in these prospective reflections, another imperative, or one might say another criterion. Just as the candidate countries have committed themselves to settling in a negotiated manner the relationships with their neighbours (treaties formalizing their border limits, from the outset, democratic relationship between national majorities and minorities, which the steps taken in the framework of the Stability Pact have furthered in an effective manner right from 1994), similarly one cannot conceive of a strategy of Pan-European rapprochement without the concerned players working to achieve it in a concrete manner. It needs to be recalled once again that 60 per cent of the distance in kilometres of the present borders of Europe dates back to the twentieth century and that Europe is, from this point of view, the newest of the continents in its geopolitical configurations. It is, therefore, a matter of the highest priority that borders be stabilized.

A first stage in the formation of a European mosaic would consist in settling the most serious among the bilateral disputes affecting antagonistic couples. Poland and Germany, then Poland and Ukraine have shown the way, just as Hungary and Rumania have decided to put an end to their obsessive face-off, favourable to extremist postures. But the list of matters waiting to be settled is a long one: Greece/Turkey, for one, which everything seems to separate since at least 1453, despite the Lausanne System of 1923, whose effects extend from Bosnia to Cyprus, the predetermined framework for a potential extensive confrontation. Then there is Turkey/Russia over Caucasia; Armenia/Azerbaijan, which are adamant over their respective positions, despite the efforts of some diplomats of the Minsk Group; Russia/Baltic countries; the Albanian question; uncertainties over the future of democracy in Serbia where some day the choice will have to be made between a micro-imperial nationalism (as if 'Serbitude' involved the domination by non-Serbs, particularly in Kosovo) and a modern, open and European identity.

Solving these often structural disputes through the path of diplomacy is a matter of priority for political Europe if it is to stabilize its approaches: facilitation, mediation, incentives, conditionality (of economic aid) and projection of military forces, encompassing also the humanitarian objective. In many fields, the interests of Europe clash with those of the United States which wishes either to jettison European interventions or, what is worse, to ensure their failure (as in Bosnia) in order to enter into the fray later and draw some degree of prestige out of handling them better. Effective intervention in crises is imperative, if political Europe is to achieve geopolitical maturity. It is necessary again to move away from an indifference which is characteristic of prosperous societies or from intellectual lethargy, both of which nurture the recurrent reproach of helplessness. The models for organization of the continent are of value only if they result, first of all, from the application of a diplomacy of the movement.

To do this, it is necessary to extricate ourselves out of the excessively Cartesian constraint of the 'all or nothing' attitude to accept a 'blurred geopolitics', laying stress less on the final borders of political Europe than on interdependencies. There should be a respect for borders and treaties of good neighbourliness, as also for the progressive nature of the practices of integration, by concentrating more on the processes of rapprochement than on final hypothetical limits. It is manifestly necessary to put in an effort of imagination to overstep and overthrow the classic concept according to which 'the politics of States is found in their geography'. It is more correct to consider, on the contrary, that the geography of Europe lies in its politics, that is to say in what the Europeans decide to make of it, in a realistic manner.

CHAPTER 6

Europe Tomorrow, between the Centre and its Peripheries

(GEOPOLITICS II)

To decide on the borders of Europe,
we have to look at geography,
keep history in mind
and settle the matter politically.

HUBERT VEDRINE (just before the European Council at Helsinki, 9 December 1999)

THE TRIPLE HELSINKI COMMITMENT

IT was a truly triple commitment that the Heads of State and Government made during the meeting of the European Council held at Helsinki on 10 and 11 December 1999 under the chairmanship of Finland. Putting an end to all differentiation between the two groups of applicant States, European leaders chose to start negotiations for membership with twelve countries of central, Baltic and south-eastern Europe. They were given the same starting position, within a single framework, initiating a kind of diplomacy of the regatta, since the moment of arriving at the goal, namely the date of full and total membership, would depend on the merits of each and the pace at which it was able to adapt itself. The membership process was designed to be inclusive, the applicant countries having to adhere to the values and objectives of the Union such as spelt out in treaties.

This enlargement council, symbolized by a family photograph which attracted attention, has confirmed that the future European Republic would also be based on the principle of solidarity. This has been noted by Brosnislaw Geremek, Poland's Minister for Foreign Affairs, himself a historian who unfailingly reminds his official interlocutors about his work on the exclusion and the poverty of the medieval West, to back up the validity of the cause that he is promoting. The element of solidarity is indeed manifest in the opening up of the European Union to a series of States which, though densely populated (the twelve together contain 46 per cent of the population of the Union), are still in the process of economic transformation (their gross domestic product is barely 7 per cent of the total of the GDP of the fifteen, and their per capita income is just 30 per cent of the average of the Community).

By acknowledging that the commitment made in 1963 with regard to Turkey, remained relevant and by accepting the official candidacy of this country, the issue of the final borders of the European Union, which for long had remained in the background, has now been revived and forms the subject of lengthy comments which are more in the nature of polemics than well thought out propositions. In opposition to a current of thought largely inspired by the Christian Democrat stream which advocates an enlargement limited to Central Europe, there is the more secular, modernist stream which favours a less culture-oriented and more geopolitical concept of a Europe that would constitute a power base and would be capable of encompassing in its fold Europeans of Muslim culture and/or religion. This is now an openly debated matter, even if the debate is not a public one. It is desirable that the call made in the European Parliament in October 1999 by the President of the European Commission, Romano Prodi, former President of the Italian Council, be heard. He said:

> I have asked the European Parliament to conduct a vast debate on the map of Europe. Which are the borders, which is the 'soul' of Europe?

What form should be given to strengthened co-operations? What decisions should we take with our southern Mediterranean neighbours, with Russia, the Ukraine, Turkey?

One can sense that the anxiety to define the final perimeter reflects a more basic preoccupation, that of the need to define the political significance that Europeans lend to their collective enterprise.

Europeans have at last underlined their determination to develop an autonomous capacity to take decisions and 'wherever NATO as such is not engaged' to launch and to conduct military operations led by the European Union, in response to international crises. This process will prevent unnecessary duplication and will not imply the creation of a European army. The approach adopted is not. It involves more that of being in a position to deploy, by the year 2003, and within sixty days, and then supporting it for at least a year, a military force consisting of fifteen brigades, i.e. fifty to sixty thousand troops capable of conducting peace-keeping missions or missions for restoring peace.

A NEW MATURITY IN EUROPEANS

The evidence of these decisive political commitments can be discerned in one specific synchronous event. When, on the promised date of 1 January 1999, a single currency was ushered in for the first nucleus of eleven members, many sceptical observers, particularly in the United States and in East Asia, were astonished. By making the Euro the second currency of reserves in the world, Europeans completed a part of their programme of integration through the market. The time lag between the economic and monetary headway and the lack of convergence in external political action has thereafter appeared more blatantly obvious. It has been important, therefore, to lay stress on a common policy for security and external action.

The tragedy of Kosovo, the fourth episode in a Yugoslav war of succession deliberately provoked by nationalist forces and factions desirous of conserving their power, of cultivating their myths and imposing an archaic concept of political relationships between nations, presented a major political challenge to democratic nations. The tensions and disagreements that arose in the western Balkans at the start of the last decade were only fuelled by the war, itself prepared by manipulating history and arousing the nationalism of resentment. This latter was kept alive by an alienated intelligentsia and an irresponsible political class, including among its components some open minded personalities, who, with their more modern outlook, were expected to take over the reins, but this did not happen. This ethno-nationalist ideology of an age gone by is seen as being fundamentally anti-European, with the result that right from 1991, when an entry into Europe was proposed to the authorities of the Yugoslav republics, the only response received, prior to the ethnic cleansing operations, was the sound of canon fire. The western Balkans have proved to be the antithesis of the idea that Europeans had formed of Europe. Backed by pubic opinion, anxious to fulfil their duty to intervene in the internal affairs of successor States incapable of ensuring a minimum of security to their nationals, European leaders have had to involve themselves, as in Bosnia-Herzegovina, on the diplomatic, then the military, and finally the economic fronts. There has been a change of attitude in the British ruling class with regard to European construction. This strategic choice will reach its completion with the adoption by the United Kingdom of the single currency whose financial role in London is already that of a key player in the international foreign exchange market. This makes it easier to plan a European capability for the military and non-military management of crises, a field in which the United Kingdom has an acknowledged expertise, resulting from its historical heritage as a recognized power and its imperative of an orderly settlement in Northern Ireland. Similarly, the political mutations in Germany, symbolized sometimes, from too geographical a point of view, by the transfer of the capital to Berlin, have led to an explicit search for normalization. Considering that it is the third greatest industrial power in the world, it becomes a legitimate candidate for a seat as a permanent member in the Security Council of the United Nations. This country is eager to display its central position in the European continent, which means simply that it expects to act as one of the major powers in Europe. External intervention, including through military force, is no longer taboo as long as it takes place within a European and Euro-Atlantic framework. As has been noted by the historian Rudolf von Thadden, entrusted with the co-ordination of the Franco-German dialogue within the government of Chancellor Schröder, 'the idea of a powerful Europe is a cause of fear in Germany more for historical reasons. But the idea is gaining ground that Europe has to be strong militarily, commercially and culturally. The French can conceive however more easily than the Germans, of a Europe less dependent on the United States' (in *Le Monde*, 30 November 1999). In other States such as Italy and Spain, a comparable evolution has taken place. In short, it has now come to be taken for granted that the Union, led by the foremost among the countries that are its members, has to contribute towards peace and international security, in accordance with the principles of the United Nations Charter, by undertaking to restore peace and order in the lands situated at its fringes.

There is another element which has induced some countries closely bound to the United States to risk undertaking an action leading towards greater autonomy. The spring 1999 war over Kosovo was the first occasion, after the Atlantic Alliance was forged, when the latitude taken by the American authorities with regard to the lines of command during the military action launched by NATO, took their European allies by surprise. The British stance is largely an outcome of this trend.

The recurrent crises in the western Balkans affecting neighbouring countries which are interested in becoming members of the Union, have contributed a great deal towards modifying the enlargement strategy of the Union. The approach which aimed at tackling the membership in successive waves, which was still the standard practice before the Helsinki Council, has been modified in favour of an inclusive process bringing all the applicant countries within a single framework. Five of these, moreover, are situated in the immediate proximity of the troubled zone. Finally, it has been found necessary to offer to the countries which are in a critical situation a perspective of European integration, in the form of association and stability agreements, starting with fragile Macedonia and unstable Albania. The crisis in Kosovo has revealed to the Europeans that they have to once again bring the Balkans into their mindset. The opening up towards Turkey and the encouragement given to a diplomatic rapprochement between Greece, the only Balkan country that has successfully achieved modernization through democracy, and Turkey, whose elites identify their history with European geopolitics, fit into the same global and pragmatic strategy.

This crucial situation explains the warranted insistence placed on the conditions of membership, summarized in what are called the 'Copenhagen Criteria', accepted in 1993. These are: the stability of institutions guaranteeing democracy, the rule of law, human rights and respect for and protection of minorities; a functioning market economy and the capacity to cope with competitive pressure within the single market; the ability to take on the obligations of membership, on the basis of the existing Community legislation, including the objectives of the monetary union. According to Günther Verheugen, European Commissioner for Enlargement, these criteria are meant only to confirm the political *raison d'être* of the European enterprise as being that of a commonality of identical and shared values.

What is in store for the period that will see its advent after the middle of the next decade—the first memberships being likely to take place from 2004 onwards—is a Europe of twenty-seven to twenty-eight members at least and, two decades from now a Union that has been enlarged to include thirty countries. This involves a solid control over the enlargement process and a reform of the existing institutions (modes of decision, balance of voting rights between States of very diverse demographic and economic consequence), in such a way that the candidates become members of a functioning Union and not simply of a free trade zone devoid of political acumen. What are the paths to tread?

A NECESSARY RESHAPING, AT THE CENTRE: AN ARRAY OF SCENARIOS

The acceleration of the enlargement of the Union has led to the drawing up of a series of prospective reports. The one prepared by the Prospective Cell of the European Commission is entitled *Scenarios for Europe in 2010, five possible futures for Europe* (final version in August 1999). It deals with the continent and not with the Union alone. It has for starting point the interplay between the players and the structuring factors. These factors, such as technology, economic globalization and information, influence the possible futures. The players are the forces, both individual and collective, likely to throw the balance of their weight on the former.

In the first scenario, called '*The triumph of markets*', it is acknowledged that the rule of economic liberalism and of free trade will put an end to the originality of Europe, on account of its conversion to the North American socio-economic model. It will become a vast economic space, unified through goods, enlarged to include new members (Switzerland, Iceland and Norway in 2004, Cyprus, Malta and the central and east European countries around 2005–8 and Turkey after 2007). The traditional values of solidarity and social cohesion are sacrificed at the altar of short term profitability and of concentration of activities in a small number of dominant regions. Europe then becomes a province of the global world.

In the second scenario, '*The Hundred Flowers*', the paralysis of the large structures of collective life and of both public and private institutions contrasts with the dynamism of micro-activities, based on a maximum use of the new technologies of information and communication. The large European Nation States are in a situation of sustained crisis and the European political space becomes fragmented, on the bases of regionalism, local lifestyles and unofficial economies. The number of near-independent entities grows, notably when nation-regions having a marked cultural and linguistic identity, a solid economic base and direct lines of communication with the larger world, are in a position to impose their political independence, 'in the name of Europe', a superior authority which makes it possible to short circuit the affinity with the old Nation States. The fragmented Union in the interior proves incapable of successfully conducting the enlargement planned at Helsinki, which is restricted to the most developed among the Central European countries. The European institutions remain idle, the interplay of alliances and counter-alliances undermines overall cohesion and the Union, as a political project, loses its credibility.

In the third scenario, '*Shared Responsibilities*', the public player conserves a dominating role, for he has undertaken his internal reform at all the required levels (regional, national, community). This is the middle path combining technological efficiency and technological innovation, social cohesion and solidarity. Public action is concentrated on the functions of implementation and of facilitation while new players flourish (NGOs, regions, civic societies). Performance is thereby increased and inequalities are contained. The Union will consist of twenty-seven members at the end of the next decade at the cost of a veritable public debate on the common political project of Europeans. True, around a dozen new requests for membership will be presented (East Europe, the

Balkans) but the unity of vision having been consolidated once again, new reforms are possible. On the strength of the success of its reforms, Europe is heard on the international stage as an advocate of multilateral institutions, of sustained development and of human rights. In this scenario, reform has come from the top.

In the fourth scenario, '*Societies of creation*', a profound transformation of the economic and social systems peculiar to an industrial society takes place while giving preference to things immaterial, notably the environment and the factor of sustained development. This is done through the introduction of accountability in ecological matters (taxes on pollution) and human accountability (taking account of human capital, through the recognition and the financing of new types of activities, situated outside the logic of the market). European economy, unsettled by the negative reaction of international markets in the face of this revolution, gives a solid base to its services, notably in the sectors of knowledge and of creativity, of tourism and the protection of the environment. But the introvert trend, linked to this radical reform, acts as a deterrent to any active external politics; the enlargement is restricted to a small number of countries (in 2010, the Union has only twenty-two States and negotiations are on with some others). 'On the horizon of the time of the "Europe 2010 Scenarios", it remains impossible to say if this post-modern Europe is about to pave the way for a planetary "immaterial renaissance" or if it is simply withdrawing from the realities of the world.'

The last scenario, 'Turbulent Neighbourhoods' is characterized by a great deterioration in the economic and social situations in the neighbourhoods of Europe. Public opinion forces the imposition of a defensive policy, akin to that of the besieged citadel. This obstructs any internal reforms and leads to the return with gathered momentum, of Nation-States. Networks proliferate which are linked to ethnic guerilla warfare, to terrorist groups and to organized crime, and they become difficult to control. The situation in Europe deteriorates further when the United States decides to let the Europeans shoulder their responsibilities in the matter of defence. Priority is given to the creation of a European Security Council, entrusted with confronting threats to security. The enlargement of the Union finds itself greatly reduced and integration advances only in the fields of security and of protection of borders. But this regressive trend spills out of the European framework and characterizes the overall world system 'which is in the process of drifting, in the 2010 decade, into a logic of non-co-operative withdrawal'.

This assembly of imaginative scenarios leads to fairly clear conclusions. Among these is the necessity for reform in public operations, for adapting the employment markets and the social security systems in order to renovate the European social model, the imperative of regulation on the global scale, the refusal of dissidence on the part of the rich regions which are beneficiaries of the growth emanating from the progress of European construction and globalization, the urgent necessity of forging relationships of confidence with the countries neighbouring the European Union based both on concrete economic and societal elements, and on a constant political dialogue. All this can be done only after the common political agenda of the Europeans for the coming decades has been clarified.

The other reports deal with more specific matters. The Quermonne report, drawn up under the auspices of the French Commissioner for Planning and completed in October 1999, is focussed on institutional reforms. It makes seven proposals: the appointment of a European Prime Minister for five years; the setting up of a Permanent Council for general matters, working with a Commission focussing on its function of making political proposals, backed by some agencies; the creation of a Council of Foreign Affairs and a Council of Defence; qualified majority voting being made the standard practice instead of the unanimous voting; the strengthening of the powers of the European Parliament at Strasbourg; the creation of a 'constitutional pact', a charter summarizing the seven hundred or so articles of the treaties of the Union, reducing their number to about thirty; finally the establishment of a 'political centre of gravity' enabling the countries which have advanced furthest in the way of European construction to act, via informal councils, on the Euro-II single currency model. Indeed a vast programme for the next intergovernmental conferences (known as the IGC).

The report prepared at the request of Romano Prodi by the Commission composed of the three wise men, Jean Luc Dehaene, Richard von Weizsäcker and Lord Simon of Highbury, was handed over in October 1999. It relates to the 'institutional implications of enlargement'. It starts off with the manifest observation that the institutional structure of the European Union was designed in the fifties for a Community of six members. It concerned at the time an original construction which has served Europe well. It is partly thanks to these institutions that the political, social and economic relations between the States and societies of western Europe have undergone fundamental transformations in a peaceful and balanced manner. The basic elements of this structure must obviously be conserved. Today however, it is clearly apparent that this system no longer functions as it should in a Union with fifteen members. The question that automatically arises is whether these institutions can effectively serve the interests of a Union which could, in the near future, encompass twenty-five to thirty and perhaps even more members. Since the fifties, successive treaties have, it is true, adapted the institutional framework, but no attempt has been made to undertake a total reform. Now we must, sooner or later, take up this challenge.

The Commission of wise men is pleading for an in-depth reform of the Union, before the next enlargements: the drawing up of a basic treaty decided upon unanimously and thus stabilized (restricted to general objectives, principles and orientations), supplemented by separate treaties, open to amendments. It recommends the strengthening of the powers of the President of the Commission, of making qualified majority voting the rule, of re-evaluating the relative importance of the Member-States in the decision-making process, of using with care the flexibility enabling an intensified co-operation between the States that have progressed further in the path of integration, without allowing the bonds to become overstated.

The report of the think tank on the 'long term implications of enlargement: the nature of the new border' (November 1999) was written under the Chairmanship of Giuliano Amato, at the conclusion of a research conducted jointly by the Robert Schuman Centre of the European University Institute of Florence and the Prospective Cell of the Commission. It brings out the necessity of safeguarding the growing diversity of the Union without affecting its cohesion while recalling the cardinal necessity for a shared political identity—political values and the rule of law, tolerance, mutual confidence and equal treatment towards subjects. It lays stress on the necessary solidarity enabling the present Union to integrate poorer countries, with a positive impact on the global competitiveness of the enlarged Union. Finally it recommends a common immigration policy, not restricted to the simple policing of the new borders, but which would partake of a strategy of reciprocal development with the eastern and southern neighbours.

The report drafted by Jacques Attali, 'Europe 2020, for a plural Union' (July 1999), recommends that institutions be reformed before any enlargement of the Union which, according to him, would have at least thirty-five members, or even forty-one, by 2020, including Turkey and Russia (as also Montenegro, Serbia and Kosovo). Failing this, the Union would be nothing more than a loose assembly likely to get bogged down: 'instead of giving a military dimension to the European Union, we would be giving an economic dimension to the Atlantic Alliance'. He describes five possible futures: an unlikely Federal Union; a Union of sovereign persuasion, falling back on its nations; a loosely-knit Union, enlarged without any substantial modifications in the rules of working and, therefore, threatened with paralysis; an Atlantic Union, the Union being, particularly for the candidate countries, simply an 'annexe' of the Alliance; finally a plural Union, which is preferred by the author, enjoying a multiform and polycentric power, in a network, organized through in-depth reforms (a new treaty, a closely-knit Commission; executive agencies; an increased budget to cope with an enlargement cost estimated at a thousand billion Euro for thirty-five members and double that amount when including Russia, the Ukraine and Turkey; finally, an enlargement conducted in accordance with 'the granting of progressive rights for dissociating the membership of the Union from the rights attached to it by linking the exercise of rights with the fulfillment of duties: no rights without duties', as a general principle for entry into the plural Union). The subsequent enlargement would no longer be subject to the same rules as the earlier ones for with them the Union will change its nature.

It is fortunate that this range of scenarios produced in 1999, endeavours to conceive of the Union as it would be a generation from now. It needs to be emphasized that there is a new awareness of the fact that a vast enlargement radically changes the nature, not of the initial political model of Europe, symbolizing peace, democracy and a culture of compromise, but of its mechanisms and its concrete effectiveness. According to a classic principle of systemics, one remark needs to be made: the Union that the countries of Central, East and south-east Europe will join will no longer be the same as that for which they are candidates today, by reason of their candidature itself. Of these various observations, we can retain the fact that reforms are indispensable in the coming years. We should also note the legitimate anxiety of the founder countries and of the few major States which have joined them (United Kingdom, Spain) to be in a position to work within a 'strengthened co-operation', a dynamic version of the 'hard core' ('Kern Europe') proposed in September 1994 by two German Christian Democrat leaders, Karl Lamers and Wolfgang Schaüble.

The commitments confirmed in Helsinki in December 1999 on joint external and security policies, on the basis of the pooling together of the capacities of action of the major States, are a first step in this direction. Beyond this stage, a long reading of European history underlines the extent to which it is important to ensure that the major countries, those availing of independent capacities for action and influence, are able to draw upon visions and formulate joint stances. They have to avoid at any cost the return of clientelisms and of partial alliances and counter-alliances, even disguised, which would be fatal to the European geopolitical project. This is also undoubtedly the only means to prevent a surreptitious division of work being carved out, devised in some circles in Washington, which visualize for the Union the sole economic role of a 'banker' (for instance, for the financing of the 'reconstruction' of the western Balkans and from the year 2000, of a Near East finally rendered peaceful). The strategic decisions, on the other hand, would be nearly exclusively incumbent on the Atlantic Alliance and on its main leader. It is, indeed, not the calling of the Union to be a sub-contractor.

It will become imperative for the main players who were the originators of the Union and those who have joined them in their own national interest, to undertake a reshaping strategy. The driving force of European construction stems out of its conforming to the interests of the basic configuration of the European geopolitics of yesteryear and of tomorrow: the nation and its expression as a State. As the British Prime minister indicated on 29 December 1999, nations, if they are to be reckoned with, must 'develop new paths of collective action'. And by way of a warning to isolationists, he adds: 'to adopt a negative attitude towards Europe, to cut ourselves off from all influence in the main alliance of the continent would be pure perversity, the very negation of our national interests in the name of patriotism'. The reshaping will, undoubtedly, not involve new judicial texts, but rather 'practices', joint actions by States and societies, themselves prepared through the setting up of convergent visions and positions. This work can only be done by a restricted group of countries desirous of advancing in order to respond to the dual challenge of the management of the peripheral regions and the formation of an alternative pole having a world-wide reach. It would probably be useful to remember that many institutions die out of an excess of politeness.

A RECAST CENTRE, THE ACTOR FOR BRINGING PEACE AND MODERNIZATION TO THE PERIPHERAL AREAS

This centre/periphery combination of words, that I am taking the liberty of using, implies no value judgement. It refers to a state of things as they stand, as this work has intended to show, at a given moment in the long history of the continent and its approaches. Its geography is not fixed; it is even fitting to note that it is in the process of being modified, and that is, indeed, the very *raison d'être* for what all have agreed to call 'enlargement'. I mean by 'European centre', the present Union which works in fact as the current seat of the modernization which it spreads towards its provisional peripheral areas till the time that these get integrated into the central system. This latter has the advantage of seniority in institutional experience and avails of relatively greater abilities in the matter of training.

Russia, at the time in history when it was the Soviet Union, was also a centre. This centrality has shrunk, following the political, ideological and economic failure of a model that had been imposed and which was held together only by reason of the guarantee of security that it had for a time offered against what was perceived as a German threat to Central Europe. As they no longer remain one of the elements of the two poles which had dominated the world scene during half a century, the elites of Moscow dream of a European continent organized on the same model, this one also a bipolar one. The greater part of the national tradition emanating from its empire, its demographic mass (150 million inhabitants), its resources, its military power and international responsibilities (Security Council, G8, length of borders of countries in the proximity of Russia) all point in favour of this direction.

But the geoeconomic reversal that has taken place in the last decade can modify this claim to parity. In 1991, the total GNP of

Central Europe was one-third that of the Soviet Union. In 1999, it is estimated that the economic worth of the countries of the former USSR represented only two-thirds that of Central Europe. This points to a spectacular scissor effect between the growth of a country such as Poland which will be worth as much as the Russian economy in the period around 2005 and the collapse of a Ukrainian economy which, unless intensive and rapid reforms are conducted, will soon be equalled by the three Baltic States. These estimates take no account either of the share of the unofficial economy nor of the capital invested abroad and are not based on the mode of calculation established on parities of purchasing power. They underline, nevertheless, the risk of a growing gap between Central Europe, strictly speaking, and Eastern Europe. This hiatus will be further aggravated by the benefits expected from the integration of some among them into NATO and the effects of modernization linked to the membership process. New peripheries on geoeconomic bases are already in position.

It has taken the Russian elites a long time to become aware of the importance of the European Union. Since the launching of the

COMPARATIVE TREND OF THE GROSS NATIONAL PRODUCTS OF CENTRAL EUROPE AND EAST EUROPE

(*in billion dollars at current level*)

	1991	1999
Total Central and East Europe	1,012	847
Central Europe	233	377
(of which Baltic countries: 24)		
Community of Independent States	627	264
including:		
Russia	466	166
Ukraine	74	30
Belarus	25	22
Poland	73	135
Hungary	33	49
Czech Republic	24	54
Rumania	29	31
Turkey	152	206

SOURCE: World Bank, 1999.

negotiations of the Union with Central Europe, they are demanding formal bilateral consultations so as to preclude what are considered the negative impacts of the next enlargements, on Russia. They struggle to give up a defensive posture, nurtured by their earlier inability to prevent the extension of NATO to three countries of Central Europe. The Commission confines itself to the procedures of dialogue provided for in the partnership and co-operation agreement already signed. Thirteen of the fifteen points presented by the Russian party relate to economic matters. They fear that a comparative advantage will accrue to the applicant countries as places attracting investments at the cost of Russia. They are also concerned over the effects of the Schengen Visa System on the movement of Russians and over a reduction of the market share for Russian products (including defence products) in Central Europe. The Russian authorities also have apprehensions that the rights of the Russian minorities in the Baltic countries will no longer be respected after the enlargement. Opinion polls, on the other hand, appear to indicate that the Russophobic peoples of the Baltic countries favour entry within the European fold as it offers guarantees that their rights will be respected (in accordance with the Copenhagen Criteria) as also the prospect of economic development. The response of the Union is summarized in the joint strategy concept adopted at the European Council of Cologne in June 1999, which is the tool for a sustainable strategic partnership.

Other joint strategies are being prepared which concern the Ukraine, the Western Balkans and the Mediterranean. As regards the first of these, the European Council of Helsinki has noted that

> the freedom, independence and stability of the Ukraine are among the most marked gains of the new Europe, rid of its old lines of demarcation. By its geography and its size, by the qualities of its population and its situation, along the North-South and East-West axes, the Ukraine, which occupies a unique place in Europe, is a *paramount player on the regional level. The Union* acknowledges the European vocation of the Ukraine and rejoices at its choice in favour of Europe.

Without decisively settling the matter, the Union invites the Ukrainian leaders to fully implement the partnership and co-operation agreement.

In the case of the western Balkans, the Union has suggested a new kind of agreement, known as the association and stability pacts. The fact is that these areas are not yet adequately stable on the internal and the geopolitical levels. The European presence finds expression in the setting up of two veritable protectorates, the State of Bosnia and the entity of Kosovo, aimed at restoring security. The ambitious objective of 'Europeanisation of the Balkans' strives to give these nations, crippled by a series of civil wars, the prospect of finding a place within the European dynamics. This is so also for Serbia once democracy has been established there and this nation is able to conceive of conducting normal, friendly relations with all its neighbours. This objective rests on a three-pronged strategy—economic development, democratization and respect for human rights and security—whose implementation would constitute a permanent endeavour on the part of Europeans for several decades.

Finally, the real progress achieved in the peace process in the Near East, as witnessed in the Syrian-Israeli Agreement, the formation of a viable State of Palestine and the Lebanese-Israeli agreement, are a very salutary element in an effective joint strategy by the Union, aimed at all these countries which do in fact have a stake in the European geoeconomic area.

Europe, as thus conceived of, has no fixed borders. Only the Union, as a political process, has been clearly defined, through successive decisions. Beyond the confines of its institutions are found some spheres in the process of Europeanization, a contemporary form of the dissemination of an experience in coexistence between nations, which has a more universal import. This means that one does not cease to be a European if one is not a member of the Union. It is difficult to believe that the Union as such would gain any benefit out of having its contours coincide with the undefined totality of the continent and its approaches. The geography of Europe will continue to be variable and its borders differential. It will have a centre, the Union. Under these conditions, the Union will be in a position to act also as a pole of world influence. The report of the Commission of the wise men arrives at a distinct conclusion on this matter. It says:

> The aptitude to play a primary role on the world scene is one of the driving forces of European integration since several decades. The dynamics of globalisation comes to strengthen these aspirations. An enlarged European Union will be still more capable and, hopefully, still more determined than today to play a role of some eminence within a globalised economy. Indeed, this should be one of its main objectives.

CHAPTER 7

Europe and the World: the Return of Modernity

(GEOPOLITICS III)

I cannot imagine Europe as anything
other than a great power.
Having a strong economic base.
A military power to ensure a security
whose responsibility would no longer be
left exclusively to the Americans.
Europe is also a model, for Asia for example,
of a deliberate union of peoples conscious of themselves.
And moreover a cultural influence added to social equilibrium.

KARL LAMERS (a conversation with the author, Bonn, 1995)

WHAT are the reasons today for 'constructing Europe'? After 1945, it was in order to further Franco-German interaction which would be an endeavour with a positive outcome, as well as to deal with the Soviet peril in Western Europe. The first objective remains valid in the present day in a continent which is now more open and less stable. It is important also to consolidate the European model into which so much has been invested since almost half a century. Political Europe requires in addition, to be transformed into an 'effective' power in the emerging multipolar world, even though it is not very clear how this can come about without some upheaval.

Till the period on the eve of the 1990s, political Europe, as a process, had found its reason for existence in itself. If came into being in the manner of an introvert, in the shadow of the iron curtain and the American guarantee of security. This move was the logical effect of the bifurcations of 1945–57: the historical setback to European influence as a result of decolonization and the Soviet challenge, the strategy for surmounting national antagonisms an reaching beyond the division of Germany, which has become a metaphor for the split in the continent.

Since the geopolitical mutations in the continent and the awakening to the reality of economic globalization whose foremost players, it is too often forgotten, are the Europeans (with their trade accounting for one-fourth of the gross product of the fifteen), Europe has to reflect with greater clarity over the manner in which it is hinged on to world space. I would like to show here that it is not only a question of geoeconomy but also of geopolitcs. These two factors complement the old and still valid reasons for 'making Europe', while adding on an attitude of clearer extraversion and the entry of a new scale, of a level complementary to the earlier ones.

EUROPE, A PROVINCE OF THE GLOBAL WORLD?

A first approach is of the geoeconomic kind, expressed by the word 'globalisation', sometimes even by 'market democracy' (a strange expression for any person who holds dear the democratic foundation of the Republic). This indicator is all the more essential as the new power equations between nations and Multi-State entities appear to have become defined primarily in the economic field (market shares, access to resources, control over change of every kind, innovative skill). It is also certain that the credibility of the currency constitutes one of the means of influence. This hypothesis of the displacement of the central criterion of strategic strength to the field of economy has been theorized by the concept of 'geoeconomy': Edward Luttwak, an American specialist of Roman military strategy, defines it as the transposition of the logic that comes into conflict with the field of commerce when he says:

> the old rivalry between States has taken on a new form which I have named 'geoeconomy'. In this geoeconomy, the capital drained by the State is the equivalent of the power of fire; the subsidies for development of products tally with the progress of armament; the penetration of markets with the help of the State replaces the military bases and garrisons stationed abroad as well as diplomatic influence. These various activities—investing, searching, developing and finding a market—are also the daily lot of private enterprises which conduct them for purely commercial ends. But when the State intervenes, when it encourages, aids or conducts these same activities, it is no longer the 'pure sugar' economy, but geoeconomy.

What is paradoxical is that 'geoeconomy is conducted only between countries which have put an end to any impulse of war between them', he adds. This practice benefits the States endowed with bureaucracies and elites which are desirous of promoting national (and European) economic interests, a substitute, in this hypothesis, for the diplomatic and military roles of the past. And it is true that the European Commission has endeavoured to effectively promote European economic interests, notably during major international negotiations.

The insertion of Europe within the global space is not a new phenomenon. There are dates galore to prove it. There was 1492 and the great discoveries whose impact on the awakening to an awareness of the spatial and cultural identity of Europe has been pointed out earlier. Then came the formation of colonial empires, beginning with that of Charles the Fifth who discovered, while admiring the globes of Hondius, that the sun never sets over them, from Seville to Manila, via Acapulco and Cartagena of the Indies. Then again 1884 and the adoption by the Conference of the International Postal Union of a division of the planet into twenty-four time zones, preceded by the progressive adoption of the metric system from 1791. Mention may be made also of the treaties of Tordesillas when, right from the end of the fifteenth century, the Papacy divided the world into two spheres. The two dominant powers of the time, Spain and Portugal, were given the mission of evangelization, inciting the others to interfere. Or again the Congresses of Berlin of the end of the nineteenth century, dividing the Balkans, followed by the whole of Africa. The crisis of 1929, the giving up of the gold standard by the United States in 1971, and the Mexican financial crisis of 1994, were also global phenomena, to say nothing of the two world wars.

Europe is and will remain a major player in world economy along with the United States, Japan and East Asia (despite the crisis that set in 1997). It will account for 25 to 26 per cent of the world's gross product on the threshold of the century. This is equivalent to a little more than that of the United States, two and a half times that of Japan and probably as much as that of East Asia. The least growth in the economy of European countries forces enterprises to innovate or to seek out new external markets. These begin moreover at the doors of the Union, in Central Europe, a durable reserve of growth, as well as in Russia, if the political system and the rule of law finally gets consolidated there.

It is customary to contemplate the crossing over to the single currency from the point of view of future European clients. Now, the success of this currency will lie also in its ability to become the other major currency of reserve in the world. It is learnt in this context that the Central Bank of China is getting ready to decide on a more varied composition of its reserves. While the economy of the United States accounts for 27 per cent of the world's production and 20 per cent of the total trade, the American dollar is used in half the international commercial transactions as well as in 80 per cent of the financial transactions. According to an estimate made by the Federal Reserve Bank of New York, 60 per cent of the reserves in foreign exchange in the central banks of nations are to be found in Dollars. The States will set about diversifying their credits and make significant transfers from the Dollar to the Euro. Some American economists (such as Fred Bergsten, Director of the Institute for International Economics, Washington, the *Washington Post*, 16 April 1998) consider that this transfer would be in the bracket of 500 to 1,000 billion Dollars. According to the Chief Economist of the Deutsche Bank, the Euro will be to the Dollar what the Airbus is to the Boeing. Finally, a number of States will link their currencies to the Euro, these being Switzerland, Norway, Poland, some others, as well as the fifteen countries of the Franc zone and, at the tail end, probably Russia, which at present is linked to the Dollar.

THE AMERICAN MIRROR

A second approach of the Europe/world dialectics is a more directly geopolitical one and leads us to examine first of all the core relationship with the United States. After having favourably viewed the formation of the common market at the height of the cold war, it was able to guarantee the maintenance of its influence after 1989 considering that unified Germany remained within NATO. The requirements of security of the nascent democracies of Central Europe also enabled this organization to continue to exist. The countries, ranging from Hungary to Kazakhstan, that had converted to the market economy, became a field of investment for American firms. Contrary to what is generally believed, they have invested more in these countries than German firms. Fearful of the Munich syndrome and with a view to extricating themselves once and for all from an in-between 'median' situation, caught between unified Germany and Russia. The countries of Central Europe, while desiring to be members of the political Union, remain deeply and closely bound to the United States. The expected strengthening of political Europe with the first enlargement goes hand in hand with a growth of the influence of the United States, relayed particularly by active diaspora (around twenty million voters on the other side of the Atlantic are of Central and East European origin).

The convergence of mass cultures and techniques, the intertwining of interests, the persistent tensions in the peripheral areas can contribute towards further tightening the bonds between Europe and the United States, under the umbrella of a NATO entrusted with renewed and widened missions (debated during the summit of the fiftieth anniversary of the Alliance in April 1999 in Washington). It is all the more possible to contemplate such a perspective as it finds supporters even in Europe, not only in Great Britain or in Ireland, but also in the medium sized States where American presence has played a role of 'equalizer of power' between European States of different geopolitical importance. A fairly anecdotal but significant proof of this is to be seen in the fact that the deliberations of the Brussels institutions are no secret to the American administration, which, it seems, is very widely consulted by a large number of Member-States before any important decision is taken. It is out of fear of isolationist decisions by the Congress, relating to the risk of negating a balancing factor in Europe, that many States hesitate to commit themselves to a truly joint security policy. If it were to succeed, including in its military dimension, how would one then justify the costly presence of American soldiers on European soil? This close bond is based also on the analysis of a world-wide situation in which the United States stands out as the one and only 'hyperpower', endowed with the main attributes of power: economy, technology, control over 70 per cent of the words and images circulating in the world, a capacity for military projection, a presence in most multilateral institutions, the attraction of its mass culture, the central role it plays in the training of the elite of the world (on this point, by way of example, two figures originating from the Community are an indicator: there are 49,537 Asian students in European universities while 2,15,496 study in the universities of the United States). Thus political Europe has little success in controlling its image abroad and any attempt at geopolitical autonomy is described, *a priori*, as doomed to impotence. European self-criticism is easily matched by America's discursive imperialism.

Another aspect of the complex relationship between political Europe and the United States lies in the place the latter gives to it in its global and long term strategy. Seen from the east coast of the United States, political Europe, 'the basic geostrategic bridge-head of America', is just a key player situated to the west of a large chessboard called Eurasia extending from Lisbon to Vladivostok. That is the postulate evolved by Zbighniew Bzrezinski, an influential expert on globalism and one of the rare American strategists sensitive to the logic of geography (1997). Being a power outside the Eurasian space, the United States, according to him, can remain the first, and the last, truly universal power only by keeping the position of an arbitrator in Eurasia. It can do this by preventing the emergence of a hostile coalition contesting the supremacy of this country, by entering for this purpose into partnerships with the key players (Germany, France, Russia, China, India), to fashion a trans-Eurasian security system. From the point of view of European interests, this thesis has the advantage of considering Europe as a player whose evolution is in full swing (notably under the impetus of France and Germany, he says). Bzrezinski points out, moreover, the lack of clarity and logic in the American position which expresses support for the emergence of a new entity in Europe 'powerful enough to share with the United States both the responsibilities as well as the burdens of planetary supremacy', while in practice, the players being unequal, the alliance still involves a hegemonic centre surrounded by vassals. He pleads for an agreement between almost equal partners, which would take note of the political fusion of Europe. He ponders, also, over the boundaries of an enlarged Europe, while hoping that after the entry of Central Europe the door would remain open for admitting the Baltic countries and the Ukraine into the Union, as well as, into NATO. The enlargement of Europe is described as an automatic growth of the influence of the United States.

As regards the autonomy of decision making in Europe, there is the risk that the enlargement might be claimed by the candidates not being integrated into NATO as a substitute for security. In short, there is a danger that the criteria and the speeds of the opening up of the political Union would be decided more in Washington than in Brussels and that the matter of the organization of Europe would be seen as a bye-product of the American strategy in Eurasia:

> Independently of each other, France and Germany are not strong enough to construct Europe in accordance with their own views, nor to remove the ambiguities inherent to the definition of these limits, the cause of tension with Russia. America's energetic and resolute involvement is required for helping to define these limits, particularly with relation to the Germans. This applies also to the settlement of sensitive problems, particularly those concerning Russia, such as the status it would be desirable to give to the Baltic republics and the Ukraine within the European system.

Finally, it is not uncommon for people to overestimate the reputation that American power enjoys in Europe, of being able to meet all challenges. Or shall we say for them to underestimate, for its part, the contribution of Europe to the influence that the United States exerts. The authoritative Henry Kissinger explains it plainly by borrowing the geopolitical metaphor of Mackinder, put in the manner of those on the other side of the Atlantic on account of his writings on Eurasia: 'Without Europe, America would run the risk of becoming an island *off the shores of Eurasia*.' The first consequence that he draws from this reinforces that of Bzrezinski: 'The geopolitical objective of the Atlantic Alliance is to prevent the centres of power of Europe and Asia from coming under the influence of a hostile country.' The second one offers prospective orientations worthy of being examined by Europeans if they grasp hold of them to lay legitimate claim to equivalent tasks to be performed, and not be content to play a subordinate role: 'The future of the Atlantic relationships does not lie in East-West relations but in the decisive role they would play by helping America to face the foreseeable evolution of the 21st century.'

A more egalitarian Euro-American relationship, in keeping with a shared leadership, will in all likelihood end up by falling in place as and when the limits of the American superpower and the growing risks of its lone *imperium* will emerge. The illusion of a durability of the present unipolar system is contemplated with lucidity by a growing number of American analysts. Two constraints are generally underlined. The exclusive military predominance of America can give rise to strategies by rival States to compete with American power. The creation of a large anti-American coalition will endanger international security. The emergence of other powers will not, therefore, necessarily lead to an environment more favourable to the United States.

An intimate knowledge of the conditions of the balance of power in European history enkindles undoubtedly Kissinger's prospective view. He constructs his vision of the interplay of powers by weighing it against the background of the large demographic, territorial and economic masses of the States mentioned as being the big players in the world: China, India, Russia, Japan, a united Europe. These make up a constellation which by itself constitutes 56 per cent of the world's population. He invokes, by way of conclusion, the desirability of a sort of *Directoire* of six members, mobilized or arbitrated by Washington. But Kissinger knows that contrary to the Congress of Vienna, which involved a limited spatial field, the rules established in the last half a century are not accepted as universal by the new players on the political scene of the world. After 1989-91, the establishment of a new order clashes with the profusion of players and interests, cultures and visions. And at this point, Kissinger notes a finding which Europeans could lean upon:

> None of the most important countries called upon to construct a new world order has any experience of the multi-State organization that we see being heralded. Never yet has a world order been instituted from the starting point of so many different perspectives nor on such a scale. No

earlier order has had to act under the eyes of a world-scale democratic opinion and in a context characterised by a technological explosion of this magnitude.

Kissinger notes in particular the difficulties Americans experience in conciliating universalist aspirations and the imperative of a durable interaction with other powers. Pushing the argument further, one may wonder to what extent *imperium* can be reconciled with the objective of greater democracy, when it is the function of the empire to reduce instability on its borders in order to guarantee order at its centre. Or then one might perceive that the American political culture, suited to a hegemonic posture, to unilateralism or to the management of a bipolar world (in accordance with a 'good/bad' grid, often convenient for masking more down-to-earth interests), would be ill-prepared to fashion an order of balance between independent poles. We see this, moreover, in Europe, since in spite of the rhetoric over an equal sharing of responsibilities, Europe remains like a sub-contractor.

EUROPE, A GEOPOLITICAL LABORATORY AND EFFECTIVE POWER

But political Europe can invest itself with real power in the world of the future. A radical geopolitical difference does indeed separate the United States from political Europe. The former acts as a single centre, even strengthened through coalitions or alliances with vassals. The model it presents is, finally the classic one in the likeness of Rome and its provinces. The latter, although excessively inward-looking, is in the process of inventing a resolutely modern configuration, with relation to the challenges of the organization of the world. It is the first and the most advanced of multi-State systems, based on the voluntary alliance of old Nation States, in which the whole adds up to more than the parts. Political Europe is the only laboratory of a multination system which is unified not through goods alone, like a Commonwealth, but through a strategy of co-operation, in the proper meaning of the word, and an aspiration for a 'Commonwill'. The most advanced experiment in integration in the world, it is not reduced to being the arena for a free exchange of goods, but is endowed with a distinct political dimension. It is a co-operative power in the sense in which the conciliation of national interests produces effects of power, as will be seen with the Euro. Nowhere else in the world do we find a system bringing together Nation-States on a contractual basis, while reconciling this with national interests. A quick glance at Asia is enough to bring out the fact that, in this part of the globe, still engaged in the interplays of pure force that were prevalent in nineteenth century Europe, a precarious balance is maintained only by the presence of an external, powerfully armed, arbitrator, the United States.

In other words, political Europe offers a modern form of experimentation in the creation of a world that is truly 'multipolar' or polycentric as Indian strategists prefer to call it. This is undoubtedly one of the messages that political Europe can offer. Being itself multipolar, it can further this mode of organization. By projecting on the outside its own internal practice, it can, in the discerning words of Hubert Vedrine, contribute towards 'civilizing' globalization. This is the close, necessary, vital bond between the unity of political Europe and its ability to carry weight in matters concerning the world.

This presupposes that the criteria of power are not limited to the classic litany of its strategic, political, economic and cultural components. Better proportioned and enriched by a fifth dimension, the ability for co-operation (the Commonwill already mentioned and borrowed from Hobbes), they describe a novel form of geopolitical democratic organization. But, as Hannah Arendt points out, strength is always a possible strength, because of which characteristic this concept is different from power which is an effective authority which ensures order, and transcends it in its capacity to create new rules. This is what political Europe is doing in its laboratory in which the 'European Republic' is being invented, a system of coexistence of Nation-States which have voluntarily accepted practices of co-sovereignty.

While becoming aware of its modernity as a 'Republic' in the making, the legacy of a joint effort undertaken since more than four decades, political Europe may find the means to come out of its ambivalent and paralysing relationship with America to which it is bound by a strange mirror effect. As one diagnosis has put it: 'America has always been the dream and the nightmare of Europe'. A dream encompassing the ideals of freedom and equality of the American Republic; a nightmare for those who dread modernity, denoted as Americanization. A child of Europe and a victorious

European utopia, the United States seems to be always ahead of its source of inspiration. Democracy was established there earlier, the recourse against the demons of nationalism and fascism, then the image of modernity after 1945 and, more clearly since 1989, all-powerful in its apparent oneness.

'Because Europe apparently no longer wishes to see in the United States the reflection of all that it can fear or hope for from its own evolution, it tends to consider the formation of a European government as an act of emancipation from America' (1954). It is time that Europeans stopped looking at themselves with vexation in the American mirror and rediscovered, finally, the unique modernity of the geopolitical experiment that they are conducting since almost half a century and in which so many others wish to participate.

According to the great historian Marc Bloch, 'there is no history of France, there is a history of Europe; there is no history of Europe, there is a history of the world'. In this history, Europe should get its voice heard anew in the light of its own experience.

EPILOGUE

In the Cafe of Europe

European unity can in no event mean anything other than unity in national diversity.

JÜRGEN HABERMAS (1995)

BETWEEN histories and geographies, it is politics which comes in to rule. Is it certain that the rhetoric of power, sustained by the elites of States and firms, will suffice to win the support of European citizens, if, at the same time the politics of the European Republic does not get constructed along innovative lines? It is not certain either that political Europe would be able to get federated under the effect of a new external threat as has been the case in the past, unless one were to place in this category the migrants who have come from the south and the east. Political Europe is a supranational institution established through treaties but devoid of its own constitution. It is therefore not a State. But it has produced a law which prevails over national laws. A flaw in democracy which has so often been denounced thus creeps in, in the form of this discrepancy. The real risk is that the control by the citizen may be replaced by the logic of networks, interests and lobbies which exert their pressure to ordain rules which end up by getting the better of the classic modes of drawing up of laws and by leading to the fragmentation of public conscience. This trend has been clearly pointed out by Jürgen Habermas, when he pleads for the drawing up of a European constitution, offering a legal and legitimate framework for a process of dissemination of information between citizens (1995).

It is probable that with the passing of the years, some signs of a European identification may become more visible, through a greater exchange of the arts and of creations, through the opening up of national education to give it a new collective dimension, through the propagation of the knowledge of different languages likely to promote inter-communication and through an increased commitment by the media which, for their part, have remained too nationalist. Even if these spaces of communication, which we know have been at the basis of national awareness, were to be set up, the question of political expressions would remain. In these signals and channels would be discerned, at the same time, a well-founded historical and cultural base.

Europe has invented the cafe, a place for debate, for communication and for reading the newspaper which, since the eighteenth century, has become the daily prayer of modern man. It was, undoubtedly, for a long time reserved for the elite whose successors continue, not undeservedly, to take the lead in European affairs with the clear-sightedness and the limitations of enlightened despots. A symbolic space of dearly conquered freedoms, a friendly nook whose atmosphere is saturated with common preoccupations, the cafe and its variants, the appropriately named 'Pub' or 'public house', or then the *Weinstube*, is a metaphor for public space. The multiplication of these free and public spaces in Central and Eastern Europe strikes the visitor even if each township of the continent does not display its 'Cafe of Europe'.

'The public space' is not simply a space for the circulation of economic or cultural goods, of judicial norms and of political decisions whose establishment has advanced rapidly since forty years in an often voluntarist manner. It is a symbolic space within which there is an exchange of discourse, mostly contradictory, between the different social, religious, cultural and political players that society is composed of (J. Habermas). This is the way that the classic, democratic nations works, under the effect of adult franchise and the clash of conflicting opinions relayed by the media. Now, there is no European public space as Europe is neither a State nor a nation nor even a place of deliberation and of public exchange of arguments. That is why there are no European citizens.

At the point at which we find ourselves in the European journey, it may be felt that the 'Euro revolution' (J. Boissonat), a primarily political decision, will have an impact on the formation of a European political space, understood as being a place for the exercise of power. The modes of management of national public finances are already being subjected to the vigilance of the other States (as an example, the heated exchanges between the German and Italian Governments over public deficits and the solidity of the Euro). A common mode of technical as well as political regulation should be applied, having a considerable social implication. Finally, the relationship with the reserves in other currencies of the world should be overseen. This will oblige European leaders to specify their objectives.

On these foundations, it will be possible to construct the Union in the best of events as an act of will, not as a depiction. The risk remains nevertheless that this political space would be controlled by a coalition of national bureaucracies, buttressing each other with intersecting legitimacies, and freeing themselves of the democratic delegation on which traditional political legitimacy was based.

To construct a European legitimacy, a Europe that people could conceive of as other than the hope of a state of well-being and a succession of reciprocal constraints, it would be necessary both to discuss and to make suggestions.

To make suggestions. In the construction of a political space, one might reflect less on the making of Europe than on the tasks to be accomplished. On the functional plane, why not suggest the formation of European parties, an election to Parliament on regional bases, a clarification of the procedures, the wagers and the roles through European political debates, and the making of a public assessment on Europe by all national Parliaments? Why not follow up the intuitions of Jacqes Delors, who has suggested that the election of the future President of the Commission be made from lists presented by political parties, in all transparency and by fully emulating the models of the projects? What is important here is to bring to the surface the general interest and to promote the legitimacy of choices of orientation. Finally, why not reflect on the emergence of a veritable 'single market social economy' whose national versions have proved their worth but which are being eroded by global networks, at the risk of transforming Europe into a vector for ultra-liberal globalization without any counterbalance? Is it believed that through these moves European citizens will make some sense out of it all?

On the geopolitical plane, when will an action programme be devised by nations gathered together, which, endowed with adequate instruments, could lead to joint actions? The time for an inward-looking Europe, finding in itself its reason for existence, is past. A new identity will be born out of an extrovert conception of the project, as a response to simple questions: what is European civilization still capable of giving to the world at large? What do we have to say to the world? In the promotion of the European geopolitical model, a system of cohabitation between nations, a laboratory of the multipolar world in the making, a new path has been explored.

To discuss. As a beginning towards the formation of a public space, a long term undertaking, we have to rework some bases (common values, Human rights, nation), to discuss also about differences and divisions, not in order to carve out identical, uniform and artificial visions but in order to bring into play the unitas multiplex which can create the new pluralist European identity, ready for self-criticism, conscious of ambivalences and open to the plurality of the world. The old identity, according to Edgar Morin, was 'democratic and imperialist and concealed this dual identity behind the seductive veil of its cultural spirituality; it was based on the certainty of possessing Reason and Civilisation'.

If we have been able, since 1945, to get nations to live together by a better management of conflicting interests, we have now to facilitate reciprocal knowledge, organize a kind of cohabitation of values, of depictions, of symbols by way of respectful communication of singular identities and differences in the visions of the world. As the philosopher Vladimir Jankélévitch asserts (*Traité des vertus*, 1986):

> democracy is neither consensus nor agreement, but the art of managing disagreements in a civilized way. It is therefore not enough to assert the dialectics of unity and of diversity to point to European identity. It is above all important for societies committed to spaces where there is free circulation of images and words, to not overstep boundaries but rather to respect them. There will be no public space without acceptance of otherness.

Teachers, researchers and intellectuals, trusts, forums and above all, political parties (social democracy which will soon be gaining a majority in political Europe, is lagging behind in this matter and has to catch up with the more active Christian democracy; it should mobilize its militants to attend to the implementation of European propositions), all have a duty, in this respect, to act both as guides and those who shed light on the path.

Bibliography

Arendt, Hannah, *Penser l'événement*, Belin, 1989.

Braudel, Fernand, *Grammaire des Civilisations*, Belin, 1963; Arthaud-Flammarion, 1987.

Bzrezinski, Zbignew, Le grand échiquier. L'Amérique et le reste du monde, Bayard Editions, 1997.

Deubner, Christian, 'L'Europe idéale de l'Allemagne', in *Revue d'études comparatives Est-Ouest*, no. 4, 1996.

Drevet, Jean-François, *La nouvelle identité de l'Europe*, PUF, 1997.

Duchene, François, *Jean Monnet: The First Statesman of Interdependence*, New York, 1994.

Emerson, Michael, 'Redrawing the Map of Europe', Public Lecture at the London School of Economics, 19 November 1996.

Foucher, Michel, 'La fin de la géopolitique, réflexions géographiques sur la grammaire des puissances', in *Politique Étrangère*, 1/1997.

———, 'L'Europe centrale et les Unions européennes: la double différenciation', in Revue d'études comparatives Est-Ouest, no. 4, 1996.

Foucher, Michel, et al., 'L'Europe dans l'espace-monde', in *L'Europe dans le monde du XXIe siècle, Aspects économiques. démographiques, stratégiques, in Le Mouvement Européen—France*, La Lettre des Européens, hors série no. 3, June 1997.

Foucher, Michel (ed.), *Fragments d'Europe, Atlas de l'Europe médiane et orientale*, Fayard, 3rd edn., 1998.

———, *Les défis de sécurité en Europe médiane*, Fondation pour les Etudes de Défense, Collection Perspectives Stratégiques, 1996.

———, avec Gilles Lepesant, Matei Cazacu, Catherine Durandin et al., *Transitions géopolitiques dans l'isthme Mer Baltique-Mer noire*, Fondation pour les Etudes de Défense, Collection Perspectives Stratégiques, 1998.

Foucher, Michel, and José Ignacio Oyarzabal, *Visiones de Europa*, Madrid, 1995 (also in English).

Fremont, Armand, *L'Europe entre Maastricht et Sarajevo*, Reclus, 1996.

Gartonash, Timothy, *In Europe's Name: Germany and the Divided Continent*, 1994 (French Translation, Gallimard, 1995).

Gowan, Peter and Perry Anderson (ed.), *The Question of Europe*, Verso, 1997.

Habermas, Jürgen, *Reply to Grimm*, in Gowan and Anderson, 1997.

Hobsawm, Eric, 'The Invention of Tradition', in E. Hobsawm and Ranger T. (eds.), *The Invention of Tradition*, Cambridge University Press, 1983.

Knafou, Rémy, *Vermeer, mystère du quotidien*, Le Musée miniature, Herscher, 1994.

Kissinger, Henry, *Diplomatie*, Fayard, 1996.

Lalumiere, Catherine, *Rapport sur la communication de la Commission 'L'avenir des relations l'Union européenne et la Russie' et le plan d'action 'L'Union européenne et la Russie: les relations futures'*, European Parliament, 12 February 1998.

Lefebvre, Maxime, *Le jeu du droit et de la puissance. Précis de relations internationales*, PUF, 1997.

Lepesant, Gilles, *Géopolitique des frontières orientales de l'Allemagne*, L'Harmattan, 1998.

Mendras, Henri, *L'Europe des Européens, Sociologie de l'Europe occidentale*, Gallimard, 1997.

Morin, Edgar, *Penser L'Europe*, Gallimard, 1987.

Sauzay, Brigitte, *Retour à Berlin*, Plon, 1998.

Smith, Anthony D., *National Identity*, Penguin Books, 1991.

Vedrine, Hubert, *Les mondes de François Mitterand*, Fayard, 1996.

Wilson, Kevin and Jan van der Dussen, *The History of Europe*, Routledge, 1993.

Wolton, Dominique, 'La nation', in *L'Esprit de l'Europe*, Flammarion, 1993.

Entre mondialisation et nations, Quelle Europe? Semaines sociales de France, Bayard Editions/Centurion, 1997.

L'Europe, '15 Regards pour comprendre', *La Lettre de l'Antenne sociale*, no. 2, April 1998.

L'Union politique, vite mais comment? Actes du colloque de la Gauche européenne, National Assembly, 11 December 1997.

La social-démocratie dans L'Union européenne, Débat entre Alain Bergounioux et Marc Lazar, Les Notes de la Fondation Jean Jaurès, no. 6, December 1997.

Réflexions sur la politique européenne, par Karl Lamers et Wolfgang Schaüble, CDU/CSU-Fraktion des Deutschen Bundestages, Bonn, 1 September 1994.

La Lettre des Européens, Mouvement Européen-France, *passim*.

Scenarios Europe 2010: Five Possible Futures for Europe, Forward Studies Unit, European Commission (Gilles Bertrand, coord., Anna Michalski, Lucio R. Pench), July 1999.

Europe 2020: Pour une Union plurielle, Rapport au Ministre des Affaires étrangères (Jacques Attali), 19 July 1999.

Implications institutionnelles de l'élargissement, Rapport à la Commission européenne (Richard von Weizsäcker, Jean-Luc Dehaene, David Simon), 18 October 1999.

Rapports sur les progrès réalistes par chacun des pays candidats sur la voie de l'adhésion, European Commission, 20 October 1999.

La réforme des institutions européennes, Rapports au Commissariat au Plan établi à la demande du Ministre délégué aux affaires européennes (sous la direction de Jean-Louis Quermonne), 26 October 1999.

The Long-term Implications of EU Enlargement: The Nature of the New Border (Final report of the Reflection Groupe, chaired by Giuliano Amato), 11 November 1999.

Conclusions de la présidence, Conseil européen d'Helsinki, 10 and 11 December 1999.

Index